African
Heritage

AFRICAN HERITAGE

BY EMORY ROSS

DRAWINGS BY JEANNE McLAVY

FRIENDSHIP PRESS · · *NEW YORK*

Copyright, 1952, by Friendship Press, Inc.

Dedicated affectionately
to my wife
Myrta Pearson Ross
and to our three children
Elizabeth, Roger, and Rachel,
who have shared with me
African friendship and affection

Acknowledgment

No acknowledgments for a book like this can ever be adequate. For it is about people, and nearly all the people one has ever known contribute to it. In my case, too, there have been scores of organizations, in Africa, Europe, and North America, that have enabled me to meet these people. I name but one, to which I owe most: the Christian church, its agencies, its members.

There are 63 individuals, however, who by their recent writings and their direct response to our appeal for aid have made immediate contributions to this book's content. I give their names and express here, as I have to them, my profound gratitude:

L. K. Anderson, J. A. Angus, Donald H. Baker, Miss Norma Bloomquist, Edgar H. Brookes, K. A. Busia, Thomas M. Campbell, Daniel A. Chapman, Andre Clerc, Robin R. Cobble, H. Wakelin Coxill, Charles L. Crane, Moses O. Dada, E. R. Danielson, W. Scott Dickson, S. N. Eliufoo, A. J. Faust, George Flora, H. M. Grace, E. W. Grant, L. B. Greaves, J. W. Haley, Bishop Bravid W. Harris, J. Maurice Hohlfeld, H. D. Hooper, Mrs. Norman A. Horner, Miss Millicent Howse, J. D. Rheinallt Jones, Chester Jump, Miss Lorena Kelly, F. L. Laubach, Julius Lewin, H. C. McDowell, W. S. Martin, Z. K. Matthews, Hoyt Miller, S. M. Mokitimi, John Morrison, E. M. K. Mulira, R. K. Orchard, Miss Annie Parker, Alan Paton, F. D. Patterson, Ray E. Phillips,

Acknowledgment

Kenneth H. Prior, Mrs. W. F. Pruitt, Darrell Randall, John H. Reisner, W. O. Rindahl, E. Bolling Robertson, Miss Kate Rutherford, Walter Schutz, L. W. Slifer, Eugene L. Smith, Miss Mina Soga, Bengt G. M. Sundkler, Channing H. Tobias, John T. Tucker, Archbishop L. G. Vining, M. A. C. Warren, Quintin Whyte, E. F. Wilkinson, and Max Yergan.

Two competent friends have given special aid in the preparation of parts of the writing which follows, and have my sincerest thanks: James Cavin, experienced Africanist, and Miss Florence Gordon, of New York. The sense, scrutiny, and endless encouragement of my wife I can never repay, though thanks be endless. Without such loyal and efficient aid as given by Miss Clara L. Bentley and Mrs. Janet Holroyd Vergoth in research, production, and other ways, the manuscript could not have been done. Leslie C. Sayre, a long-time colleague in Africa, is equally good as editor and stimulator in New York. To these friends and to the Friendship Press staff I offer my deepest thanks.

If the book has some worth, the aid of a long life's friendships and partnerships is the reason. Its shortcomings are mine alone. For the gifts others have so generously given I shall be always grateful.

Emory Ross

New York, N. Y.
MARCH, *1952*

Contents

Contents

[v]

Foreword

Africa is searching. Africa is being searched. The searchers from within and the searchers from without are not all after the same things. It follows that many of the things found and the means of finding are not pleasing to all of the searchers.

They are all, in a way, looking for a heritage. Traders are looking for profit—for themselves and their children. Hunters are looking for trophies—for their museums and their houses. Scientists are looking for knowledge—for their institutions, their students, mankind. Settlers are looking for homesteads—for their children's children. Governments are looking for power, prestige, protection. Nearly all are looking for something to pass on—a heritage.

For what are Africans looking? I hope we shall glimpse at least a bit of their searchings in the pages that follow. I am grateful to many Africans who have allowed me, in the last forty years, some sight of their searchings. Those searches are for hosts of things. But the heart of the search today is in one word: life.

All people want life—the traders, the hunters, the scientists, the settlers, the governments. But for Africans today the search for life has circumstances, qualities, and possibilities seldom, perhaps never, found before in combination by any group of 150 million people. It is with these circumstances, qualities, and possibilities that this short book seeks to deal.

Africa has, on its own, developed no great new spiritual form. It has no hard shell of encrusted philosophy. It is not a secondary alloy. Spiritually and humanly it is primary material.

This primary material, in our day, comes suddenly and directly into contact with Christianity and with a Western society whose finest building is on Christian concepts. Many Africans, sensing the beauty and fullness of true Christianity and glimpsing some proofs of its power in society, see in it life in new dimensions. They want such life.

They do not have to struggle out of the containment, for example, of Islam, to embrace and enter this new life. They have the advantage of a primary people. They are relatively free spiritually in the wide search for life, new life, fulfilling life. From their fathers' common, basal heritage, which all peoples have shared, they start a search for new life, a new heritage for their children.

Thus far, it is in Christianity that they see their greatest hope. Some 21 million have chosen it. They are seeing that in Western life it has done much. They see, too, that Christians everywhere have records of failures, that Christianity has therefore not brought our generation the fullest heritage possible. Out of the earlier common heritage that all peoples have shared, can Africans now both gain and contribute to the new desired heritage?

No group so primary and so large has ever had just such a chance as Africa has in today's world. For it is not only Africa that is in change. The whole world is struggling for change. It is seeking some of the lost good communal qualities of the common past. Those qualities are implicit in God's Fatherhood and man's brotherhood. They are explicit in Christ's teaching and example. They are dangerously deficient in the West's heritage today. Western man's primal wholeness is nearly gone.

In such an age the past and the future African heritage may have its special power.

Emory Ross

New York City
MARCH, *1952*

*African
Heritage*

Chapter One

HUMAN RIGHTS IN AFRICA

TO BEGIN THIS SHORT STUDY OF AFRICA AND THE CHRISTIAN church with talk of human rights, as if it were a difficult and basic problem in the spread of Christianity, might have seemed strange a few years back. Perhaps to some it seems strange even now. In the past, the church could go preach and teach in Africa without any special fear of being hindered by questions of human rights, for Christianity was thought of as the chief establisher of those rights.

Our Western world has rather prided itself on its observance of human rights. It has been wrong in such pride. Western practice of human rights has in many ways and in many places been far from our profession. Nevertheless, we have had charters and laws to protect human rights. Our governments were, in large measure, founded on and committed to the application of human rights. Many of us have taken these rights for granted. We have counted on their almost automatic extension to other parts of the world that the West has undertaken to govern.

However, the subject peoples themselves have not been convinced that the Western governments are trying to give them full

[1]

human rights. The insuperable truth is that one country cannot *give* human rights to another country or people, even if it wants to. It can apply its own human rights to its colonial peoples with a sincerity that may give it considerable satisfaction and perhaps a feeling of moral rectitude. It can, if it tries hard and wisely, help create an atmosphere in one of its colonies favorable to what it conceives to be good human rights. It can try to demonstrate them and educate the people for them. Or, if it has the physical force and the desire, it can take away many or perhaps all human rights. It can do certain things *about* human rights, but it cannot acceptably *give* human rights to another people.

Indeed, the history of modern colonialism provides evidence that the more sincerely and earnestly a governing nation educates for human rights and declares in favor of human rights for a colonial people, the more rapidly those people develop a cohesive and self-assertive attitude against the governing nation and for their own self-government.

This is not an anomaly, nor is it base ingratitude. It is not evidence of the weakness or failure of a well meaning governing country, though it may seem so at first glance. It is, in fact, a triumph of that country's principles, including the principle of human rights. It shows that the colonial people have caught and understood the principle and want it for themselves. They have seized the right to demand their rights.

In such a situation, the more sincerely a governing nation is committed to human rights for itself, the less effectively it is able to justify their denial to its subject peoples. It becomes impossible to attempt forcibly to deny to or unduly retard for another people the right to choose their own human rights—an initial right that is inseparably linked with self-government.

This dilemma—or success—of a colonial government that sincerely believes in human rights for all and finds its colonial peoples suddenly demanding self-government is considerably heightened in our day by Communist campaigns. Such campaigns often use and share other forces going their way against "capitalist exploitation" and toward "freedom" for colonial peoples.

This Communist method of infiltration, of spurious but for many people plausible identification with deep human yearnings for freedom and a better life, of secrecy and deceit, of terror, torture, and death, has created fear and resentment in the West. This fear has, at least for the time being, somewhat strengthened the forces of reaction and oppression in non-Communist countries, particularly against minorities and nonconformists who, rebels against the injustices from which they suffer, can always be labeled "Communist" or "subversive" or "traitor." North America's decade of living in a kind of foggy fear of communism and of totalitarianism in general has resulted in a threat to and some actual curtailment of human rights in this powerful "free" continent. The same thing has happened in Europe, rather more drastically.

One effect of this has been the creation of additional conflicts in Africa. Many Africans are beginning to feel that the attainment of human rights, growing partly out of their traditional culture and partly out of the better of their contacts with the West, and of self-government within a new world relationship is really possible. Simultaneously, the threat of communism is causing some countries in the West to cling desperately to all they think they possess, overseas colonies included, for what they consider their own and the world's good. The urge to hold Africa is powerfully reinforced.

European and other spokesmen have publicly and repeatedly said that Africa is probably Europe's greatest economic asset, even

[3]

its salvation. Belgium's wartime and postwar financial stability is largely due to the Belgian Congo, where it has developed what seems to many the best integrated economic system in Africa. Very large new economic undertakings are in progress in other parts of Africa.

Most of these have either current or future value for Africans as well as for foreigners. But there is little if any confidence among Africans that they are to share the benefits in any equitable proportion. Their rights—their broad human rights—in all these things going on in and concerning Africa seem to them uncertain, perhaps irreparably jeopardized. Much of what is happening is hidden from them by distance, ignorance, or design. It is little wonder that an increasing number of Africans tend to lash out more and more against all things white and foreign, the church often included.

TEN FACTORS IN HUMAN RIGHTS

The following ten factors have their special importance in Africa today in this broad, basic matter of human rights:

1. Many within the ruling group in Africa are not so complacently sure as some once were that they can *give* their package of human rights to, and have it accepted by, the Africans.

2. However, they do not feel wholly willing to trust Africans to choose, formulate, and apply human rights themselves.

3. The mutual confidence necessary for both groups to make their maximum contribution in choosing and formulating human rights is to be found rarely, if at all, in Africa today.

4. Many in the ruling group fear a Communist-type subversion of human rights, no matter from what source these rights may come, if the African is given any major degree of political responsibility "too soon."

[4]

5. The ruling group's long-demonstrated sense of the need and "right" for European control of Africa is thereby strengthened.

6. More and more Africans think this to be at best mere rationalization, and at worst sheer humbug and hypocrisy. Many of them have seen forced labor and other forms of economic exploitation under colonial regimes. They have experienced the "divide and rule" technique that has often appeared to them subversive of their best interests. Some thousands of Africans have now seen the outside world, through service in two world wars and as students and workers abroad. They have seen its vast inequalities, its prejudices and discriminations. They have seen its great fear of communism despite our alleged confidence that the Christian West has all, and infinitely more, than communism can offer. Many Africans, after seeing and experiencing this, are convinced that the West has not demonstrated all the answers. They may even suspect that we inwardly fear we cannot find all the answers.

In any case, the Africans want to share in finding the answers. When they feel barred from a process of real sharing, they swing, quite humanly, toward complete self-assertion. They say they want to make all the answers—self-government *now*. That was the feeling and that was the slogan that in February, 1951, won forty-eight out of eighty-four seats in the new Gold Coast Legislative Assembly, which inaugurated the most advanced modern undertaking in mass self-government in the whole of Africa thus far.

7. The church is tied up with all this because of its history and past actions. In its history it cannot deny being originally a foreign importation into Africa. In its actions it has too often, in the African view, remained a foreign importation. The

[5]

reasons for this are complex and powerful, as may be more clearly seen later. We shall seek to show that in many ways the Christian church, despite its mistakes and human weaknesses, has made the greatest of modern contributions to African life—spiritual, intellectual, social—many of them directly aiding the material improvements that Africans are gaining. But many Africans feel that the church in a number of areas has not done all it could to assure to Africans either the full use of Western human rights or that basic right of all peace-loving peoples: to choose, formulate, and administer their own human rights.

8. There are perhaps two principal reasons for this judgment. One is that neither the Protestant nor the Roman Catholic missionaries are felt to have come out promptly, unequivocally, and strongly, in many instances, on cases of injustice, exploitation, forced labor, and other human abuses. Therefore the churches are counted as more or less lined up with the reactionary elements in groups responsible for these abuses.

9. The second principal reason relates rather specially to the Roman Catholic Church in Africa during the past century. (a) The Catholic Church is felt to have done little in the past century, except where strongly stimulated by non-Roman pressure, to improve the temporal and educational status of the mass of African people and to aid them to the fullest enjoyment of the Four Freedoms. (b) The Roman Church has made common cause with certain economic groups by huge investments of church funds in their colonial businesses and has developed exclusive and dominating political ties with certain governments. These practices are regarded by Africans—and oftentimes by others—as repressive, exploitative, and otherwise inimical to certain basic human rights.

[6]

10. It seems probable that informed and thoughtful Africans would agree that the Protestant church is not generally to be condemned with the Roman Catholic in those two respects. The Protestant church has been the great pioneer, stimulator, and backer of education in all its forms in nearly all parts of Africa. Neither its principles nor its practices lead to amassing of large reserves of money for capital investment in colonial or other enterprises. But the fact remains that, since both are "Christian," it is the Christian church, the Christian religion, that is condemned. All Christians suffer for the faults of some. That applies equally to a variety of failures within the Protestant community itself. It is true in a wider sense also: Christianity in Africa suffers from the sins of all Christians, of all Westerners, of all whites everywhere. Christianity in Africa is still too much a Western, a white, a foreign thing. Its failures and shortcomings in Western, white countries are becoming ever more clearly known to Africans.

Because of these several factors there is, within the minds of a larger and larger number of influential Africans, more concern and more questioning than in previous decades about the Christian church's effective support of human rights. One might make a strong presentation of the decisive influence of Christianity in favor of human rights in Africa, but skeptics could point to what seem to them shocking failures of the church in this field.

The church is here in its universally difficult position. Whenever and wherever its performance does not match its profession, it is more harshly judged than any other human agency would be under the same circumstances. This is understandable and probably fair. The church is of divine origin, and if its human leaders fail, they ought, many feel, to be judged more strictly than the erring leaders of a secular body. This seems to be the feeling even of men who do not believe in God. Illogical, that may be, but there it is. And there that feeling is in Africa. Every failure of the Christian church seems a failure ten times over. For from the church, which promises most, the greatest things are expected.

So it is that at the very beginning of a study of Africa today and of the Christian's relation to Africa, there is placed this broad question of human rights that touches every facet of human life.

INDIVIDUAL VERSUS COMMUNAL GOOD

More of the world's people have talked more pointedly and constructively about human rights on a world scale in these past six years than ever before in human history. This is partly a measure of the recognition of the dangers to human rights that are abroad today. But it seems to me basically and principally due to the positive Christian philosophy, and a certain amount of encouraging practice, regarding: (a) the sanctity and immortality of the spirit and personality of man, and (b) the Fatherhood of God and the sonship and brotherhood of man. While no religion or culture has a monopoly on the concept of human rights, there seems to be clear evidence from both Christian and non-Christian sources that where Christianity has exercised its best influences there are to be found many of the best developments of human rights.

These developments have been largely though not exclusively in the West. They include the growth of individual freedom, the protection and rewarding of individual initiative, the creation of our industrialized society, and the improvement of living standards. These processes themselves have, however, frequently curtailed human rights, and fresh battles to guard them have ensued.

But in these as in all battles it has seemed not enough merely to guard the old ground; fresh frontiers have been required both for their own sake and the better to protect the old. An offense has seemed the best defense. Hence in the West a constant struggle goes on to broaden the meaning of the term "human rights" from its earlier individualistic concept to a wider base that would include high benefits for the community as well. In a sense, though much too simply, that seems to sum up our world struggle today, a struggle to get the highest good both for the individual and for the community. The West gets much of its drive for this from the Christian gospel.

Africa is drawn willy-nilly into the very midst of this struggle under circumstances that have few if any parallels in history—indeed, no parallels involving so large a mass of peoples.

The traditional and "untouched" Africa south of the Sahara is almost wholly an animistic, communal society.[1] Its animism is essentially like that of all past animist societies, our own included. Animists believe that all objects in nature, animate and inanimate, are inhabited by souls, spirits that may exist in a separate state; that practically all phenomena in nature are caused by these spirits; that food, shelter, health, happiness, progeny, and survival itself are dependent on gaining sufficiently the benevolence of these spirits, or at least on placating, deflecting, or neutralizing the malevolent among the spirits.

This animistic religion, which is clearly a handicap in many ways in the new life and world into which African peoples are being drawn, is challenged by Christianity, by Islam, by secularism, and potentially by communism. Thus far, numerically at least, Christianity has made the most progress. But animism is

---

[1] Communal and communalism are used here to refer to primitive social organization where land and goods are possessed in common and the individual is almost wholly subordinated to the community.

[9]

still the mass religion of Africa, and it still exercises its practically complete control of the relatively untouched masses in Africa's communal society.

The communalism of this society—the subordinating of the individual to the community—controlled by the animistic religion, was first challenged six or eight decades ago by the old, extreme individualism of the West. Individual Africans were then and still are invited and urged, even compelled by economic and other factors, to exercise individual choice. In the primitive communalism that nearly all societies have experienced and that is Africa's present way of life, individual choice is generally quite subordinated to group control, as in marriage and other intimate family matters and a great variety of other things. By today's stimulated and stepped-up exercise of individual choice and resultant individual action, the communal control in African society is being weakened.

Christianity has played a powerful role in this break-up, openly challenging animism, which is the binding and controlling force in African communal society. Its desire to strengthen African individuality has perhaps been better understood than its purpose to help the African couple that individuality with responsibility in the larger Christian community. The result of the Christian struggle for the hearts and allegiance of African animists is not yet decisive for the future of Africa. It is not yet decisive among any people.

The fact to consider here, however, in relation to human rights, is that the closely-linked struggle of Western individualism against African communalism, and of Western Christianity against African animism, has pulled 150 million Africans into perhaps the most confusing situation that has ever been faced by an emerging primitive society.

Consider only four of the principal elements in this situation:

1. Africans are being asked—and forced—to change their whole way of life faster than any comparable group in human history.

2. The change originally demanded three or four generations ago, and still largely required, is from a primitive communalism to an advanced individualism.

3. But in the midst of this demand and change, its initiator, Western society, has suddenly shifted its direction from extreme individualism to some kind of advanced and more productive communalism.

4. The African, shaken in his belief in tribal control by the forces of Western individualism and eager to gain the strengths of that individualism, is checked in mid-flight. If the powerful West has lost faith in all-out individualism and seems to seek a saving communalism of some sort, where is the African to take position? To find balance? To assure his future? Has he, in his still powerful communalism, a better soil and rootage for himself and for others than has Western individualism? Or is he, in a new sense, to be a slave to the West, to follow, but in speeded tempo, its thousand years' trek from communalism to individualism and around to a saving communalism, only to arrive late at each stage and suffer the consequences of such lateness? Or can the African move from a primitive communalism to a form of advanced community having a sufficient degree of individualism in it, without paying the penalties of adoption and then rejection of the more extreme individualism from which the West is recoiling?

In addition to these four social elements, consider also seven of the principal spiritual elements in this matter, remembering that, in Africans' minds, the spiritual is never separate from the social and other factors, as it is likely to be in the thinking of Westerners, but that the spiritual permeates and illumines all the other elements.

1. Christianity is everywhere effectively challenging African animism, and Christianity thus early has won the public allegiance of about 21 million Africans.

2. Christianity has introduced and continued the vast bulk of Western education in all Africa south of the Sahara, sometimes with and sometimes without the financial or other aid of governments.

3. But Christianity has come almost entirely as a Western article, fashioned and flavored by some forty generations of Western thought and experience that are almost wholly foreign to Africans.

4. As a Western article and in the Western tradition, Christianity is functionally dissociated to a very great extent from other Western articles that Africa is receiving and wants: Western science, economics, land use, technology, industry, political structure, and other things.

5. But in the African tradition religion is not and simply cannot be dissociated from these other aspects, all aspects, of life. Therefore when these other aspects of Western life cause what the African feels are inequalities, hardships, and injustices, his experience with animism tells him that Christianity, as the religion of the people who are responsible for these things, is at bottom to blame. And when that religion, represented through the church, hesitates or refuses to denounce and work against these abuses publicly and clearly, and sometimes gives what seems to him the very lame excuse that the "spiritual" church cannot, as such, battle these other concerns

[12]

that are "secular"—a distinction unknown and unacceptable to the African in his traditional society—he is profoundly shocked.

6. It is little wonder that many an African in this situation finds himself torn between two beliefs: either (a) the Western Christians are not telling the truth about an accepted division of things spiritual from things secular, which makes no sense to him, but are deliberately ranging themselves with those exploiters and oppressors who are of their own race and color, to further dominate the Africans; or (b) Christianity cannot be much of a religion if it supinely admits that it has little or no control over the total lives and actions of its members. Animism can do more than that! So can Islam.

7. This disillusioning experience of the African regarding what he supposed was the universality of Christianity as a controlling force in Christian society, this incredible split between "spiritual" and "secular," is heightened by three other splits that millions of Africans constantly see: the division between Roman Catholics and Protestants; the divisions among Protestants; and the division between white and black. More is later said about these three tragic divisions, but on no page of this book and in no future thinking about Africa let us ever forget them and the other and even more important division already mentioned—the generally-applied Western separation of the "spiritual" from the "secular." These are the Four Horsemen that ride hardest against Christianity in Africa.

HUMAN RIGHTS UNDER ATTACK

There is another powerful reason why Christians can no longer take for granted the fact of human rights in Africa when they go out to preach and teach and try to live Christianity in that

[13]

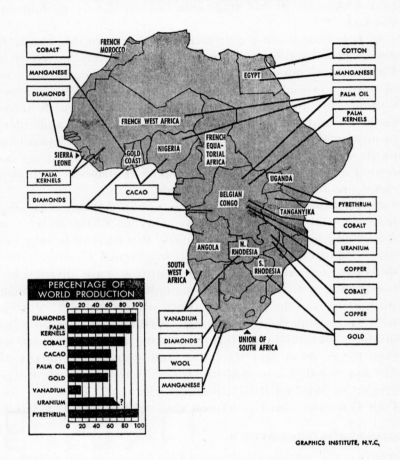

AFRICA'S MAJOR PRODUCTS

COBALT
FRENCH MOROCCO
MANGANESE
DIAMONDS
COTTON
EGYPT
MANGANESE
PALM OIL
PALM KERNELS
FRENCH WEST AFRICA
SIERRA LEONE
GOLD COAST
NIGERIA
FRENCH EQUATORIAL AFRICA
PALM KERNELS
DIAMONDS
CACAO
BELGIAN CONGO
UGANDA
PYRETHRUM
TANGANYIKA
COBALT
URANIUM
COPPER
COBALT
COPPER
GOLD
ANGOLA
N. RHODESIA
S. RHODESIA
SOUTH WEST AFRICA
VANADIUM
DIAMONDS
UNION OF SOUTH AFRICA
WOOL
MANGANESE

PERCENTAGE OF WORLD PRODUCTION

	0	20	40	60	80	100
DIAMONDS						
PALM KERNELS						
COBALT						
CACAO						
PALM OIL						
GOLD						
VANADIUM						
URANIUM					?	
PYRETHRUM						

0 20 40 60 80 100

sensitive continent. It is the massive attacks, from varied sources, on the whole concept of human rights in world society. If in the past six years more has been said and printed about human rights than ever before in so short a period, it is because our generation has witnessed these staggering attacks.

Socialism, industrialism, laborism, cartelism, statism, nationalism, racism, fascism, Nazism, Marxism, collectivism, Stalinist communism—these and many other "isms" have professed to fight for some or all aspects of human rights. Protestantism and Romanism have also been among the forces that have fought for human rights, each in its own way. But the result of the struggle among the various forces in our own generation has been to bring about perhaps the greatest threat in history to human rights.

In this connection, the Christian family must face the painful and humiliating fact that, in the West as in Africa, Protestants and Roman Catholics seem to be using more of their time and strength against each other than appeared to be the case a generation ago. This growing conflict involves at many points basic elements of human rights. In some places in Africa, notably in "Latin" Africa, whose governing countries in Europe have overwhelming majorities of Roman Catholics in their populations, Protestant Africans and Protestant foreigners devote unhappy time and energy to the struggle against political, economic, and social forces of containment and threatened expulsion directed against them by the Roman Catholic Church.

Periodically throughout the past twenty-five years or so, there have been Roman Catholic prelates and lesser spokesmen who have voiced and published their aim to force all Protestant missionaries out of one or another of these African areas. In Italian territory they practically succeeded. In Congo Belge some years ago they carried on campaigns of physical persecutions, with the

[15]

tacit consent of local authorities, who refused to intervene. After six or eight years of the persecutions, the Congo Protestant Council amassed such documentation for the government authorities in Congo and in Belgium that orders were issued to judicial and political officers to step in and stop such actions. In Portuguese territory, the Vatican alliance with the authoritarian regime has exercised all its power to prevent any expansion of Protestant work, although it has not yet been able to extirpate it.

This sustained effort, quite consistent with Roman Catholic doctrine and practice, when it has the power, to dominate and apply the police force of the state against the Protestant religion and to drive it out, is a threat to human rights wherever and under whatever form it shows itself. It should be an occasion for penance within the Christian community. It is one of the reasons why Protestant missions cannot take it for granted, as they formerly seemed to do, that human rights will be established and protected in Africa without any special concern on their part.

All of this adds up to the sobering fact that millions of Christian men and women professing the clearest and most universal and dynamic principles man has yet discerned in the field of human relations have in some respects failed in establishing those principles among their own people and among the so-called underdeveloped peoples of the world.

This ought to bring us to the perception that all people are underdeveloped, without exception. No people have yet developed all the potentials for good that are within them. Many North Americans are very smug over our development in this continent. It is good in a number of ways. But others, not only in Africa, see our failures, our "underdevelopment." Likewise, we see theirs.

We can see the Africans' backwardness quite clearly. We call

Africans underdeveloped. From a certain point of view that is correct. But if the Africans call us underdeveloped as Christians, can we deny it? If they say we are underdeveloped in racial attitudes and practices, what is our answer? If they feel we are underdeveloped in peace, are they wrong?

Colonial spokesmen continue to cite the Europeans' suppression of intertribal wars as one of the great contributions of Western civilization to Africa. But it seems at least arguable, although there are no earlier figures for proof, that intertribal wars for a century or two before the European partitioning of Africa did not involve as many men, as much bloodshed, and as much treasure from Africa as did the two world wars of our single generation. We must also add to the debit side the African lives lost in the slave trade, foreign imposed, and in the wars and bloodshed of "pacification" resulting from forcible European domination of Africa.

Foreigners point to the great contribution made by the Western education of Africans, and rightly so. But the vast majority of Africans could say, "What education? We have none, nor our children." For nowhere in Africa are more than a small minority getting education as yet. In a good many areas, those who are getting it suspect it, as at present offered, as a device to secure their improved manual and clerical services for a stepped-up exploitation chiefly benefiting foreigners.

In African areas where there is a small minority European resident group, the colonists talk a good deal about their rights in the government and future of the country. They have lived there for two or three generations; their children and grandchildren are there. They have brought in Western capital and know-how. Their share in the present economic development of the colony is felt to be much larger than that of the African tribes-

[17]

men—themselves foreigners in that they had earlier moved into the areas and pushed the former inhabitants out or down. The rights of the more recently arrived European settlers to stay and share largely in the rule of the land are therefore argued to be historically, culturally, and economically as good as those of the Africans.

I should judge that many Africans, sensible and adaptable people that they are, would be willing presently to acknowledge the need of such co-partnership in the developing and governing of their homelands. But the unilateral assertion of rights is not generally the best way to establish confidence and trust, and to solve complicated human, economic, and political problems. This is particularly true in situations of racial, economic, and political tensions and fears, where no agreed, common, and understood code of human rights exists and current laws and procedures are largely the importation of one party to the dispute.

The *need* for cooperation and sharing by both parties in Iran's oil-related development was clear and basically agreed. But the *right* of the Irani unilaterally to determine how this need was to be met was bitterly contested by others concerned. In this case, the foreign minority protested a "right" of the local majority. In "settler" areas in Africa, the local majority protests the "right" of the more recent foreign minority. Law may be on the side of the foreign minority in both cases. But until law and human rights reach a generally accepted identification in a given community, the almost universal human and spiritual impulse seems to be resistance to such law as does not conform to the locally accepted pattern of human relations and human rights.

A good many aspects of foreign law in Africa today seem to Africans not to conform to the realities of life nor to the rights of man. It seems unrealistic, for example, for foreign law to require an eye witness to a murder. Africans agree that murder may be committed by magic, by evil spirits, by possession. The actual perpetrator rarely can be seen. Even if a man is seen to do the actual killing, he may not be the murderer at all. He may be possessed by the real killer—who might equally well have used a lion or a crocodile or a falling tree limb for the deed. These things can only be discerned by divination, by magic, by poison tests, by bone throwing. To require or even to trust an eye witness is quite illogical. An eye witness may even be really dangerous and send an innocent person to his death merely because he saw him strike the blow.

But foreign law seems to the African at times to be worse than unrealistic. It seems to strike directly at the rights of man and society. Much of African society is organized around secret age groups or sex groups or spirit groups. Occasionally in some of those groups a human sacrifice is required. There are deep-seated spiritual reasons for this. Those reasons seem dispassionate and valid, based on long experience, basic to the continued life, security, and welfare of the group and tribe. Foreign law sometimes steps in, seizes one or two, maybe more, individuals accused of "ritual murder" and executes them.

Many Africans believe that the human rights of both the individual and the group can be grievously injured by such procedures in the case of genuine ritual murders. The group is injured because, as all members and many nonmembers know, it requires such occasional sacrifice to assure its group well-being and under some circumstances its very existence. Such sacrifice is therefore a recognized human right. What kind of law is it that denies this right and kills those who uphold it? The condemned individual is injured—and killed—in a particularly unjust fashion, for he was acting solely in the interest, at the behest, and under the compulsion of the group, was not responsible as an individual, and should not be killed as an individual when he was really the group in action.

Such wide differences as these between African and foreign cultures, between African and foreign law, between African and foreign human rights, can end only through the long, slow processes of spiritual illumination—not just of Africans, but of the hearts and minds of all concerned. For though the basically conceived "rights" of man are called "human," they are in their very essence and being spiritual. The battle for human minds, the battle for human loyalties, the battle for human rights is one and only one battle: the battle for the spirits of men. Not a battle to capture and dominate men's spirits. Rather a battle to free and empower men's spirits.

In that battle the Christian gospel has no equal. Despite the human weaknesses of its followers, it is the world's greatest battler for the spirits of men, for that freeing and empowering of the spirits of men that is their right. In Africa, that right, above all, is required.

Chapter Two

THE CHRISTIAN COMMUNITY AND
MOTHER EARTH

THE GREAT CITIES OF AFRICA, LIKE THOSE OF THE WEST, MAKE
newspaper headlines oftener than the villages and farms. The
population south of the Sahara is variously guessed. Let us say
154 million. But practically all the news from this part of Africa
that reaches us in North America comes from cities whose combined populations total perhaps 3.5 million people—places like
Dakar, Freetown, Monrovia, Abidjan, Accra, Lagos, Ibadan,
Brazzaville, Léopoldville, Luanda, Capetown, Lourenço Marques,
Johannesburg, Salisbury, Dar es Salaam, Elisabethville, Nairobi,
Kampala, Addis Ababa. The combined populations of fifty other
urban centers may equal a like number. Of such a possible 7
million African urbanites, probably 2 million are fairly recent
arrivals from the country, still feeling a strong sense of loyalty
to the families and communities they have left in the rural areas.
The more thoroughly urbanized 5 million are thus only about
3.3 per cent of the population in Africa south of the Sahara. Even
that small fraction is tied really closer, spiritually and economically, to Mother Earth than are a good many of America's people
who are called rural.

Therefore, while the urban centers can under no circumstances be neglected in the services of the Christian church and in the growth of a new Africa, it is clear that the mass relationships of the church in Africa must be with the mass of the peoples of Africa's villages and farms. Furthermore, if Christianity is to root and grow in African life, it must root and grow where nearly everything else has been rooting and growing in African culture and society—in the minds and spirits controlling the lives and outreach of the millions of rural men and women in Africa.

The ideas and leadership developing in the cities are of great importance. But for a long time to come Africa will be predominantly rural. In the rural homes and communities will be initially formed the personalities, the characters, and the life potentials of most of the thousands who will move out into industry, government, education, and the other professions in their own and other lands. In such service they will largely form and guide the expanding life of Africa and its relationships to the world.

An African friend who has thus moved out into such service in African life, the Reverend Seth M. Mokitimi of the Union of South Africa, has a strong conviction on this subject, backed by intimate experience. He knows how difficult but how needed are the message and practice of the Christian gospel in the rural communal society of Africa. He says:

> The Christian church, through its missions, has been the greatest conscious force for change that has ever operated upon the life of Africans. It came to people content with the communal life which they, within the tribal group, lived essentially in exclusiveness and separation. To the African, life to be enjoyed had to be lived on the land of his birth, among those of his kith and kin to whom he was joined either by blood or by the central

[22]

authority of the tribal chief. Strangers were always suspect. The Hottentots of early South Africa calling themselves "the complete people" and the Zulus calling themselves "Abantu" (the people), each thus emphasized the exclusive nature of their close-knit tribal communities.

The Christian church came with the message of an all-inclusive community. "Whosoever will may come," was the call. It taught of the brotherhood of man and proceeded to gather people of differing clans and tribes into "new colonies," the colonies of heaven, representative of the new humanity. Around the little thatched mission church men and women forgot their tribal differences as they sang the praise of Him who died. A new and most explosive and expansive concept of community was born. In many places, still existing today, tiny houses clustered closely around the village church; a "church village" had come into being. Anyone coming into it, perhaps fleeing from the vengeful arm of cruel paganism, knew he would be accepted. The church has brought a widened outlook to rural African community life.

Nevertheless one of Christianity's greatest obstacles has been tribal solidarity. It always stood against the Christian message and influence with all its power. The individual had never thought of himself as standing alone. He and his family were part of a tribe and all his thoughts and actions were in terms of how the tribe thought and acted. He had never felt able to strike off in a new path on his own. Where the tribe moved *en masse* into Christianity the matter was easy; but where, as often had to be the case, an *individual* had to decide to hive off and cast away the beliefs of the family and tribal tradition in response to the call of the new faith, it was not easy. Many an individual was torn in the conflict, and deterred by fear of the ancestral spirits. Christianity required conversion as a personal matter, an affair between God and individual man.

In the church therefore the individual has acquired a dignity and independence quite unknown before. An individuality has

[23]

been developed which is bound to stand the African in good stead against the battering of Western civilization, and when in the large cities he has to decide for himself and stand on his own feet.

Africans' opinions would, I believe in very large majority, support Mr. Mokitimi's: that Christianity has been a tremendous force for change in African communal animistic life. It has, indeed. No change has been greater than that wrought, illumined, and continued by the Christian gospel—that is, the revelation of the love of God in Christ. An inspiring word picture can truthfully be painted of this tremendous change in the lives of people numbering millions and living all over the plains, forests, mountains, and swamps of Africa. Inspiring pictures have their place in human life. Often they show how much can be done with little when the spirit is right. But I suggest that instead of pausing too long to rejoice over past achievements, we try to see how much more is required. Let us consider how different much of that "more" must be, if this change, begun and largely developed in Africa by Christianity, is to continue toward its goal of the maximum good for the African people.

The land in Africa and the people upon it might be examined first; together they form the rural community, which Africa is. It is in the rural communities that the first and widest effects of the new and tremendous change have occurred. It is where some of the greatest problems now appear. It is where some very different and much wiser effort has to be made in Africa.

The land, for Africans, occupies the place it has nearly always held in animistic communal societies. It is the sacred, most precious, inalienable possession of the tribe. Mother Earth is held to be the producer of all life, the sustainer of all life, the recipient of all life. Land is therefore the indispensable possession of the whole tribe, for the continuity and well-being of all life. Nothing could be dearer. This is perfectly clear and logical in the minds of all the tribe.

The spirits of all the tribal members who throughout all the generations have gone before, reside in Mother Earth. Separately and together they are a powerful control of the life and destiny of every living member, of the whole present living generation, of all the members yet to come. Those spirits and Mother Earth, forming a close-knit unity with all the present living members of the tribe, are the conservators and guarantors of tribal life in all its aspects and for all the generations to come.

The spirits and Mother Earth, with all this responsibility, are conservative, seldom on the side of change. Mother Earth and all the powerful forces residing in her are believed to favor things as they were, as they are. Safety lies in tradition, in conformity. The individual or the generation that is heedless of Mother Earth, that violates the all-embracing traditions of Mother Earth, risks direct punishment, even tribal annihilation. There is little if anything worse than trifling with Mother Earth. For Mother Earth holds the destiny of all life. She is to be feared, revered, placated, and obeyed by every loyal member of every generation.

This is a power and force that cannot be "graphed" even by the West's most scientific procedures, or microphotographed, or fed piecemeal into an electric "brain" to produce a formula and a plan. But it is a dominant element in the control of all African life. It must never be forgotten by foreigners who are trying to understand and aid Africa.

The introduction by the West of the theory and practice of private ownership of land can be seen, in view of all this, as a tremendously disruptive act in African life. Even the government

[25]

ownership of land, perhaps regarded by some European authorities as less disruptive than, although intermediate to, private ownership, or perhaps in some parts as a kind of group-trust holding for the Africans themselves, is almost everywhere feared, resented, and spiritually resisted by the Africans. For a foreign and colonial government cannot be regarded by most Africans as in any sense taking the place of the close-knit and spiritually-based tribal group, or as validly acting for it—least of all, perhaps, in taking ownership of the land, the precious Mother Earth.

Where Christian missions have shared, as they generally have, in the practice of this private ownership of land for what have seemed to them the necessities of their Christian work, they have added very considerably, and no doubt often quite unconsciously in the earlier days, to the confusion of Africans regarding Christianity. The Christian gospel preaches God as the Creator of the world (Mother Earth), as demonstrating through his son Jesus his Fatherhood of all mankind and the brotherhood of all men, and his concern that *all* shall share the bounties of his love. This can easily seem to the African to be, among other things, a strengthening of his own reverential attitude toward the earth and all that it represents for mankind. This in turn can seem to be a strengthening of the concept of the communal ownership of land for the safety and good of all. Yet Western missionaries practice, and seem to want to compel helpless Africans to accept, what seems to many Africans to be the illogical, disruptive, antisocial, and downright selfish private ownership of the most precious heritage of the race.

Even where Africans are left in relatively undisturbed possession of their tribal lands, the question of the improved use and productivity of that land remains one of great complexity. Everywhere in Africa the people need better and more food. Better balance in diet is desirable, which means new and more foods to

[26]

THE LAND OF AFRICA

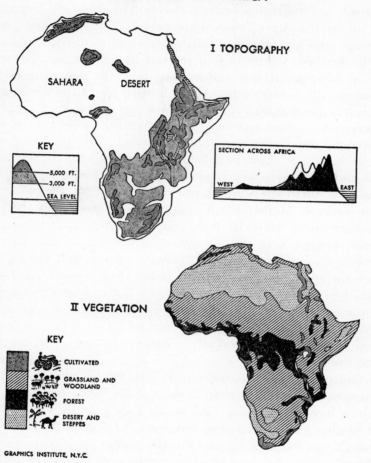

I TOPOGRAPHY

SAHARA DESERT

KEY

5,000 FT.
3,000 FT.
SEA LEVEL

SECTION ACROSS AFRICA

WEST   EAST

II VEGETATION

KEY

CULTIVATED

GRASSLAND AND WOODLAND

FOREST

DESERT AND STEPPES

GRAPHICS INSTITUTE, N.Y.C.

be grown and sometimes better cultivation of old foods. Improved seed selection and preservation are needed. The forest and grassy coverage must not be unnecessarily destroyed to provide new cultivable fields every three or four years, as in past practice. For with both a rising population and a rising diet, the denuding of the soil can bring on erosion that could in turn retard the whole agricultural and community improvement effort.

Every one of these and many other needed changes are strongly resisted by important sections of the rural African community. These changes go against tradition. There is no convincing demonstration that they will succeed physically. There is even less proof that they will succeed spiritually. Will all the powerful spirit forces in Mother Earth approve them? Not likely. In fact, almost certainly unlikely. For these controlling spirits have arranged things as they are. They have achieved a delicate balance between the good and the bad, between success and failure, between life and death for the whole tribe. Mother Earth can by no means be lightly dealt with. Much less is one to follow the lead of complete outsiders in dealing with her. What can those outsiders know about the tribe's Mother Earth, and all the tribe's ancestors whose spirits live there, and all the new spirits that are destined to come from there?

Granting that those outsiders may have "medicine" that makes these new methods seem to work successfully in Mother Earth, the African nevertheless asks, "What can they possibly know about our Mother Earth?" Nothing, obviously, he decides. In fact, their methods and medicine may be literally poison for Mother Earth.

Furthermore, he feels that the temporary success of foreign methods used by foreigners on small demonstration plots means little. Western medicine is obviously new to the ancestral spirits inhabiting Mother Earth, and they may require a bit of time to organize the opposition. The African is sure that, as in the past, Mother Earth will gain the victory for the tried methods, and the outsiders' medicine will fail.

But even in case the outsiders' medicine continues to be successful in their hands, there is no proof that it would work equally well in African hands. It might not desire to serve them as faithfully and well as it does the foreigners. Even if, by chance, it should wish to work for them, very probably Mother Earth would be violently incensed at their reliance on foreign spirits and would exert her utmost power against them. All life might crumble about them. It would be better to stick to what is proven and sure.

Thus the African reasons. The overwhelming majority of the rural people—and that means the vast majority of the African people—are not to be quickly swung to innovations in regard to Mother Earth. They distrust new agricultural methods, diversification and rotation of crops, fertilization, all the technology of an improved subsistence crop and of new cash crops that seem to Westerners so rational, desirable, and not too difficult to master.

Further, for the Africans this whole question is not just a matter of growing more crops, important and desirable as that is. In the Africans' view what is involved is *life itself, the whole of life, in its every aspect.* To touch Mother Earth in Africa is to touch life itself, the whole of life past, present, and future. It is not to be lightly or quickly done, especially on the say-so or experience of outsiders who have no knowledge of and no community with the Africans' ancestors and their own Mother Earth, and who in turn are unknown to them—strangers, who are naturally to be suspected and feared.

Even fifty years ago in Canada and the United States, farm owners with the background of a thousand years of education,

[29]

experimentation, industrialization, and individualization resisted the strange, new-fangled ideas of scientific agriculture that their sons and daughters brought back from the agricultural colleges beginning to grow up here and there across our continent. In regard to the changing use of land, rural societies do not move quickly, even when better and more profitable crops are badly needed.

Tens of thousands of Africans may become literate. Thousands may accept Western education. More and more may become proficient in Western law, medicine, industry, science, and politics. But for many of them, and for the vast rural masses of Africa in this next generation or two, some of the most difficult problems of all will center around attitudes and usages related to the land, to the all-important Mother Earth. Outsiders will be suspect. Rural conservatism will be militant.

All this brings us to the two most critical points in connection with African rural and community development:

1. The job can't be done by outsiders. It must be done by Africans who help bring to Western training the knowledge, viewpoint, sensitivity, and confidence of the African and who channel out of Western training the usable knowledge in usable form for a rising African society. Outsiders can be of help. Africans must do the job.

2. The concept of the future rural community development can be neither a slavish copy of that in the West nor a static print of African animism. It is certain to be something different from either, just as the British concept of rural community development differs somewhat from the Continental, and the North American is different from the European.

Let us consider first an element in this second point: that rural

[30]

community development in Africa cannot be a slavish copy of that in the West. This is so because of the greatest weakness that Western Christianity and Western technology (using "technology" to include all of the applications of science and of scientific experience to the whole business of daily human living) have in relation to Africa.

That weakness may be thus stated: Christianity established the base, inaugurated the modern education, favored the freedom of mind, soul, and body, and otherwise gave the greatest encouragement for the development and employment of the whole of Western technology; yet it has not continued in Western society as the illuminator and guide in the uses of that technology. The result is that those uses, many of which are misuses, have brought on in society a spiritual and social revolution of such depth and power as to threaten the whole life of man. This Western technology has so far in our generation escaped the control of its—and our—Creator. Christianity currently does not light and guide our Western life. Christianity has its compartment in Western life. It has its responsibility. But that responsibility is not generally regarded as extending either to the purposes and usages of technology or to many other aspects of Western life—that large bulk of Western life that is called secular and that is largely insulated from the element called spiritual.

This separation between Christianity and "real" life is perhaps carried further in the United States than in other parts of the nominally Christian West. The American principle of the separation of church and state has sometimes been misinterpreted to make it mean a tragic progressive separation of religion and life. This is further dealt with in Chapter Four, but it must be taken account of here, for it is a significant factor in the West's approach to African community development.

[31]

TRUE CHRISTIAN COMMUNITY [1]

Unless we of the West can regain our Lord's conception and practice of his gospel, his love as a guiding principle of all life, we shall not be able to do our best toward aiding the African in his development of an appealing, integrated, and productive African Christian community.

The African community needs a cleansing and a wholeness in its new world such as Jesus taught and lived in the needy Hebrew community of his earthly years. The Hebrew community, like the African, had its good points, and Jesus as a son of that community knew them and commended them. But he also knew its fetishes and superstitions, its reliance on forms and ceremony, the strength of its oppressions, the weakness of its love. He knew the narrowness of its tribal concern and loyalties. Even the Samaritan cousins were outsiders and despised. A good Samaritan had to be illustrated by parable. He could hardly be conceived as reality.

Today in the West we are at a stage where the ultra-individualistic free enterpriser can allege that the good Samaritan is not the true hero of that tale at all, but rather the innkeeper. It was the innkeeper who had accumulated enough capital to put up the inn and install the beds and the kitchen, and who was thereby able as well as willing to risk his capital by taking in a wounded nobody on the credit of a passing stranger—and a Samaritan stranger, at that.

It can be retorted that if the community had not built a road, developed transportation with the aid of draft animals, and organized controls sufficient to let trade and travelers get through,

[1] By Christian community here is meant that group of Christians, whether in daily touch or seeing one another rarely or never, who each in his daily, his hourly life seeks humbly and earnestly to put Christ's teaching and example into practice in everything he is called to do. No one ever succeeds fully. But it is the one who tries consciously, humbly, and ceaselessly, who is in the Christian community in the sense in which those two words are used in this book.

[32]

neither the good Samaritan nor the free enterprising innkeeper nor the man whom the thieves had felled would have had any luck at all in living their own lives or becoming the principals in one of the parables best known among men.

The individual is indispensable and is infinitely precious. It is he and he alone who has direct relationships to God. It is he and he alone who can accept or reject the invitation of Jesus Christ to follow him. It is the individual who is the most precious unit among men. But the unit is not enough. Community is equally indispensable, equally precious. Never has the concept of individual fulfillment within community been better exemplified than when Jesus taught and lived in the primitive Hebrew community. The West does not have that Christian community, but African Christians now have the opportunity of seeking to create it in Africa. Africa's success in this would bless more than a single continent. The whole world is in agony through not having such Christian community.

In a single generation, we have had the two most universal and deadly wars in history. We have experienced the successively mounting waves of fascism, Nazism, and communism—totalitarianisms all seeking with religious fervor to achieve a oneness in the world under the power of arms and the police state. The zeal of those who would unite mankind under the Christian gospel seems for the time being to have been surpassed. Can we not discern more clearly than ever that the community of Christians, the oneness of mankind inherent in the Christian gospel is the highest and most practical oneness known to man?

In the oneness of Jesus Christ even those who reject him are still among those he loves and for whom he died. They are still brothers to be sought and won, Jew and Gentile, young and old, male and female, rich and poor, bond and free. Where else is there

[33]

a oneness comparable to this, if actually practiced in truly Christian community?

It is the failure truly to practice such Christian community in the Western and nominally Christian world that has contributed most ruinously to the bitterness and despair of the whole world today. It is the true practice of that Christian community that Africa would most heartily welcome today. There is not a problem in the whole of Africa that would not be made easier of solution if only the Christians themselves, black and white, minority though they be, were practicing more fully this truly Christian community.

Christian community as our Lord taught and lived it means two things: the inclusion of *all the people* who elect to join, with never-ending concern for all others also; and the inclusion of *all the life of all the people.*

It is in this second matter that we fail most. Our real inclusion of all people who elect to join and our concern also for all others is by no means perfect, in Africa or outside. More and more, though, we accept that as our goal and slowly but encouragingly we struggle toward it in many places.

But we in the West have not really accepted the inclusion of all the life of all the people as a basic requirement of Christian community. More often than not in the West when we speak of Christian community we are thinking of the community of people, but only of a part of the life of the people. We think of such things as the congregational activity and the members' personal shares in it, of the home life of the members, of the relief and social welfare service in the community and the participation of Christians in it.

Then we begin to shade off more and more in our thinking. Politics? Yes, perhaps that might be sometimes included; maybe especially in local political affairs, when they get too bad. But state politics, and national and international? Is it not fair to say that the wider the political outreach, the more, on the whole, it escapes the illumination and guidance of the Christian community? Why? Because it has become too widespread, too global? That is really no reason. For the Christian gospel is, and prides itself on being, a global religion; indeed, it is the only truly global religion there is.

Economics? Industry? Labor? Farming? These have traditionally been regarded as private enterprise. Only rarely is the Christian community expected actively to concern itself with the illumination and guidance of private enterprise. However, now that economic problems are rather moving out of the realm of strictly private enterprise, what kind of community is gradually taking control? Isn't it the political segment of the community, the industrial segment, the labor segment, the farm segment—the so-called "power" groups? But what about the power of the spirit, on which the best of all this enterprise has been based and has grown—the power of the Christian ideal, of the truly Christian community?

Education? Science? Is it generally expected in North America that Christian community, concerning itself with all the people, will also effectively concern itself with all the life of all the people? With education, and science? We see daily the negative answer. It is becoming more and more difficult even for those desiring it to pray together in our schools.

To many maturing Africans who have come to know the West, this segmentation is irrational, even downright stupid. And dangerous. As they learn the history of the West they find, as do most Westerners, that Christianity was the soil in which this expanding and rising and lifting society of the West was nurtured. Christianity was what might seem to Africans to be, in a way, the great Mother Earth of the West—more, for it enabled man to use the powers and mysteries of the earth as no African nor other people have yet been able to use their Mother Earth.

Christianity, from this African viewpoint, provided the key that unlocked the earth's storehouse. Christianity favored and founded the modern Western education that explained the meaning of much of the wealth of this storehouse and trained the mind for ever more knowledge. Christianity gave the release from animistic superstition and fear, the freedom and spiritual courage, for science to begin its long quest of the inner mysteries and composite powers of the great natural elements of this unlocked storehouse. No other religion from animism on up has ever done this to such a degree, the African sees.

He begins to grasp how Christianity gave the leads, the courage, the venturesomeness for the formation of a society that appears to have achieved intellectual and material emancipation greater than any in history. With his fresh and spiritually sensitive mind he has little difficulty in seeing how so powerful and inclusive a religion as Christianity could do this. It is indeed a great religion. It has done great things for its believers, naturally. That is a fact he easily accepts, for to the African the role of religion in life is to guide a man's and a tribe's whole life.

But then another and double-headed fact begins to intrude, completely baffling: that only a small minority of the people of the West profess to believe in this powerful religion, and that most of those who do are not clear that it can or should effectively concern itself with the whole of life. He wonders how it is possible for this to be so. If animism, which has not done a fraction as much for his traditional society, can be the basic control of all African life, how is it that Christianity, with all its demonstrated power, is thought suitable to control only a part of Western life? And if the West can get all it has gotten out of Christianity and can still exclude and ignore that religion as a guide for the whole of life, why can't Africa, too?

For North American Christians—for all Christians everywhere —those are two of the basic questions of our time. Would we have gotten ourselves into the present terrible world situation if the first of those two questions had been answered by the West in our generation as the normal African would think it should be answered? It seems scarcely conceivable.

Now look at the second question. How can we expect our partial and faulty living of Christianity in the West to recommend Christianity to millions of non-Christian people who in this very generation have been sucked into the pits we have successively digged for ourselves? In the broadest sense, it is the individual and collective failure of tens of millions of professing Christians to make their religion the overriding power in their lives that has permitted and even stimulated the works of evil that threaten to engulf us.

Herein lies the basic weakness of Western Christianity in approaching both the single individual and the scores of millions who make up the rural communities of emerging Africa. We of the West are seldom able to do much better in helping rural Africans build an inclusive and spirit-controlled Christian community in Africa than we have done in our homelands. Sometimes our faulty Western conceptions and inhibitions may even be hindering African Christians from taking Christianity and trying to build such a Christian-controlled community. For that pattern is not very familiar to us in practice. It has novelties that we instinctively fear. We shrink from having Christianity "secularized" —a word for which, in the Western sense used here, the Africans have no equivalent either in speech or concept.

It may be, too, that, human-like, we of the West can scarcely conceive of "primitive Africans" taking Christianity and making something better of it in their combined individual-community life than we have in the West. It was easy for the educated and the economically and politically powerful people of Jesus' day to look down on the carpenter, the fisherman, and the net-menders who said they had a better gospel than the traditional teachings of the chosen people. Humility is a Christian virtue, but is it today a Western one?

At this stage in the church and mission in most parts of Africa, the Westerner is still dominant. That is not likely to continue indefinitely, but it is so today. We may not now have such power that everything we favor is done. But things are not often done that we do not favor, unless there is a split in the church and the Africans definitely break and go on their own. Then it is usually too late to get a real meeting of minds and souls between Westerners and Africans for the good of the Christian community in Africa, and excesses occur that still further stiffen Western determination to keep Christianity "pure," which means, at least in part, keeping it more nearly like our Western pattern.

But today probably more people recognize more clearly than ever before in history the power, on the one hand, of real Christianity, and the weakness, on the other hand, of Christianity's Western pattern. More and more Africans are certainly seeing this. It is not just the sins of individual Christians that give them concern, although individual failures are always a debit in every society. There is a more fundamental and baffling weakness in the West: that Christians do not seem to believe that Christianity has the duty and right—and the realism—to control the whole of the life of all its believers. It was the announced principle of its founder that it should. It has more to offer than any other religion among men. Why is it so hesitant and weak?

[38]

That is the core of the problem that Christianity faces in all its relationships with African men and women and African society today. Perhaps Africa can help us find the solution. But it can help us most only if we will freely agree that our Western Christianity is truly weak and faulty in this, that these faults and weaknesses should not be imposed on Africans, and that the growing African church may be a pioneer that can help us to find the pattern and practice of true Christian community that all the world so desperately needs.

FAMILY LIFE

In two strikingly different units in African life today there is special need and challenge for preparation and practice of Christian community: in the home and in the city. Home and city—these are almost the opposite ends of present African social structure. For in a certain sense the traditional African home is totally unknown in all but a handful of African cities. Ibadan and Abeokuta in Nigeria are examples of urban centers established before the Western invasion. Africans had true homes there, although the tie was very close with the surrounding land. A few other urban groups predated Western contact. But even those have now greatly grown in size and changed in character. And most present-day African urban centers are completely new, having been established in the last fifty years or so. A poignant phrase for the Africans—many men, a few women—who have gone to Africa's cities is that they "left home." When they go "back home" they are in most cases very changed.

Christian community must begin in the Christian home. That is the place where the wee individual's multipersonal relationships begin, where his social pattern starts to form. There the mother is the key.

[39]

But one of the greatest weaknesses of Christianity in Africa is that it has concerned itself so much less with women than with men. As seen when we deal with education, even the single women missionaries from the West, designated specially to work with women and girls, too often leave them and work principally in teaching and training boys and young men. The latter are freer and more eager. The women seem somehow duller and inaccessible. To whatever degree they are, it can be accounted for by their traditional subposition in African society, by the fact that they, the mothers, like Mother Earth, are the producers and sustainers of the life of the tribe. As such they are to be approached with the greatest conservatism and deliberation. Change, if any, must come very slowly and after ample proof that the life of the tribe will be bettered, not damaged.

Christian community is an unexcelled pattern for bettering the life of the tribe and of all men. But there are too few places as yet in Africa where continuous intensive and envisioned work is being done to establish the whole concept and practice of Christian community in the African home. This may be partly because we ourselves clearly have not done too well at this in North America.

The African home, however, has perhaps some special aptitudes, along with some major drawbacks, for development of the idea and practice of Christian community. It is the unit where this must begin. It is the unit that has contributed a good deal to animist communal society. It is a kind of human taproot of the tribal tree. There are Africans, missionaries, and others in Africa, Europe, and North America who face the African Christian home as a great challenge and opportunity in building the Christian community throughout Africa. There is a demand for greater efforts to be made there immediately by the most skilled and devoted Christians among us.

[40]

The urban centers in Africa present a problem that is more concentrated spatially than is the African home, but which is in some ways a problem more baffling even than that of the African home or of the African rural community, both of which cover the whole of the continent.

From an African social and spiritual view the recently manufactured great cities of Africa are a kind of C-bomb, made up of African fissioned material more abundant yet more precious, and more powerful, than uranium. Enormous sums have gone into the project. There are great areas of ignorance surrounding it. The fissioned material is not well understood, and is unpredictable. Much secrecy prevails. A great deal of the working is attempted by remote control, in which the C material is kept beyond what are hoped to be protective walls of one kind or another. The critical mass is as yet unknown. So there is everywhere uncertainty, tensity, even fear.

It is really a good deal like Oak Ridge or Brookhaven or Hanford or the Savannah River project. Except that in the C-bomb the fissioned material is human, sentient. It has ideas of its own. It is infinitely variable. No physics or chemistry can fully analyze it. No electronic brain can calculate it. For it has spirit. And where there is spirit, truly anything can happen.

A number of such cities are named at the beginning of this chapter. The total would run into scores. They are all growing, and their number is increasing.

The chiefest of the things that make them is money. And money, in itself, is a new and disruptive thing in African life. No mass of people can shift from communally-controlled barter to individually-gained money in two or three generations and not be disrupted—not even though they like the money.

So when this powerful element of money and the C-bomb city

[41]

are joined, African society has a real problem. The problem is made harder because the city draws hundreds of thousands of Africans of principally one group: able-bodied men. The women, for the most part, stay at home, and the children, and the more mature and old men. The homes are broken in the rural communities, and homes are too rarely built in the cities. The two principal stabilizer forces in the tribe remain at home—the older men and the women—but most of the "stabilees" have flown. And it is not to be assumed that they get stability in the cities.

There are sometimes men of a hundred or more tribes and languages in a single city. In some places they live in compounds. Elsewhere they are in awful slums. Even where housing is good and water is laid on and toilets are flushed into pipes, the social and spiritual problems remain and mount.

But because of the very concentration of humanity in these cities, the uprootedness, the bewilderment, the groping for something new and satisfying that they feel has eluded them, there is a great chance for the ideal and the practice of Christian community. It could be that through Christian community the undeniable power of the C-bomb city could be transformed and carried for spiritual and social good throughout all the land. Some kind of power is bound to come, and in increasing volume, from all these built-up city piles. With faith, and more works—beginning with the greater backing and giving of North American Christians— a good part of that output might be Christian community in the cities aiding Christian community across the land. For Christian community serves people, wherever they are and whatever they may have been.

CHRISTIAN EXPERIMENTS

Let me close this chapter with descriptions of two rural family and inclusive community experiments being made today by Christian African and missionary colleagues. These are not quite typical, for there is not enough of this kind of sustained effort, coordinated with all the other activities of the church, to warrant "typical" as a descriptive term. However, a number of the separate elements in these experiments are to be found fairly widely in Christian efforts throughout Africa.

The "experiment" feature in these examples is not to be found primarily in the Christian use of the separate elements, which, like the elements in nature, are widely present and used. Rather, it is in the effective combination of those elements to get the most power out of them separately as well as in varied combinations, under a spiritual formula both understandable and congenial to the people. This matter of making plans understandable and congenial, through practical demonstration and showing that they are based on a satisfying and inclusive spiritual concept, is of great importance in winning the people and in assuring the vitality of the effort in the future. It is the visible, satisfying, and inclusive spiritual concept that, to many Africans, seems often so strangely lacking alongside the many practical demonstrations of the material prowess of the West. It is in essence this separatism in the West between the secular and the spiritual that puzzles and, in some of its demonstrations, embitters the African.

The oldest of the experiments referred to is at Kambini in Portuguese East Africa. Here, on 1,000 acres of land, an educational center was established in 1909. Since that time, there has been a continuous and progressive effort to apply the whole gospel to the whole of life. The missionaries began with boys eager for an education. Later they took in married couples, girls, and young women. The whole new community was based on Mother Earth. Every individual had a responsibility to the land and through the

[43]

land to himself and the community, for food, clothing, shelter. Members of the community put up the buildings out of the clay, grass, stone, and wood of Mother Earth. They raised plants from which they could get fibers, prepared them, and made their clothing in considerable part. They raised the vegetable and animal food on which their very life depended. But instead of ignorantly robbing the earth of its riches and perhaps suffering famine or being forced to let land lie useless to recover its productive powers, they learned the new and varied wisdom regarding land that enabled them to put something back into the land from which they continually drew sustenance. This was revolutionary. It was contrary to the wisdom of the fathers. It went against the spirit-controlled processes of the past. It is the kind of thing generally resisted by primitive rural men and women everywhere.

But at Kambini this new approach to land, to Mother Earth, was not separate from all the rest of life—from sickness, "book" learning, community organization, recreation, seasonal festivals, marriage, home and children, worship, music, and God. It was tied up with the other new things that were also coming into the country: money (a thing very strange and disruptive in a barter society), bicycles, sewing machines, phonographs, railroads, automobiles, cameras, cotton gins, telephones, telegraphs, motion pictures.

New ideas were coming in, too, and some of these seemed very strange, including the new concept of God and the news of his son, Jesus Christ; and the idea of brotherhood and community extending even beyond clan and tribal lines—very strange indeed. But many of the new ideas and material things seemed desirable. They were introduced in simple, integrated, and understandable fashion there on the land at Kambini, and the people were able to see that they were interwoven and interdependent.

It became clear that almost all of the new material things were the result of Western man's relationship to Mother Earth. Christians believed and taught that it was God the Father who was the Creator and Giver of all these things. It was he who enabled man to develop and enjoy them. It was he who gave man power over them. That power was not in charms, nor fetishes, nor witchcraft, nor "medicine." The power was in man's simple, continuous acts day after day, year after year—acts growing out of a good heart, a developed mind, a trained hand. That was God's way of enabling man in the long reach of time to control and use all the material powers of Mother Earth—the Mother Earth that the Christians taught belonged not just to one tribe but to all the tribes of all the world.

Man's hardest job was to use the spiritual powers available to him. If he used them rightly, then the material powers were his also for the good of all men.

This is a concept congenial to the African. It is for him the clarifying, the purifying, and the infinite expanding of his animistic communal religion, just as it has been for the Jews and Gentiles through the centuries. It is the essence of true Christian community, more powerful and more satisfying than anything else human society has yet found.

The man who started the Kambini experiment in 1909 with the support of the American Methodist Episcopal Church was Pliny W. Keys, who came from Kansas "Aggie" and Baker University. He was later joined by Ira E. Gillet from Oregon "Aggie" and Oberlin College. In 1925, Julian S. Rea joined the Kambini group fresh from Massachusetts Agricultural College and Boston University School of Theology. These men, their wives, and other American men and women have worked at Kambini with Africans steadily all these years to build Christian community. They are

[45]

not interested principally in the small community at Kambini, but aim at putting the all-inclusive concept of Christian community into the hearts and minds of Christian Africans in all the villages and tribes that the Kambini influence can reach. The work goes steadily on. That fact is one of the powers of Christian community anywhere.

In 1932, Mr. Rea supplied Agricultural Missions, Inc. with an outline of the Kambini program that listed in nine packed pages about 208 elements of the new community life. Practically all of these 208 had numerous direct sub-elements not listed. For instance, one element named was "Preaching"; another was "Personal and village hygiene." Others were "Donkey breeding," "All evangelists and students learn to plow," "Better family relations—Christian homes," "Preserving the good in African life and customs," "Temperance instruction," "Drama and dramatization," "Cocoanut plantation," "Extend possibilities of self-sufficiency through simple allied industries," "Midwifery, infant care, and feeding," "Scribes—reading and writing letters for the people," "More intelligent relations with the Administrator and other government personalities," "Seed-time dedication service," "Bring *men* into more responsibility in African agriculture," "Introduction of cattle to breed for milk production," "Creating a sense of appreciation for God's gift upon which agriculture is based," "Instilling the feeling that agriculture is cooperating with God in the use of these gifts to feed mankind," "The village council," "Xitswa music adapted to Christian use," "Adaptations of dry farming and cool season crops," "Africans' contributions to the interdenominational paper *Kuca ka Mixo* (1500 circulation)," "Interpretation of the Christian religion in terms of African life, not as a European system," "Famine prevention," "Pastoral responsibility for surrounding country (normal radius

[46]

of about one hour's walk, three miles or so)," "Week-end institutes," "New methods of harvesting and stacking peanuts," "Marketing," and "Evangelists set up replicas of Kambini."

As indicated by the last element named, other centers modelled after Kambini are being established. This is one of the most inspiring outcomes of the long period of work at Kambini. For more than 40 years the center's mission team, including Africans, has been working at the comprehensive program of cultural change, agricultural change, economic change, political change, spiritual change—the change of the whole life into an inclusive Christian community of all the people and all the life of all the people.

Probably a thousand Christian centers in many parts of Africa are working in other ways on all these manifold elements of change. The elements are almost universal in Africa today, and Christianity is one of the principal forces in lifting them up. But no evangelical group, so far as my knowledge goes, has been working longer, more steadily, with more inclusiveness and a more congenial and winning philosophy of Christian community in African society than the Christian leaders, black and white together, at Kambini. They have been doing it almost entirely on slender evangelical financial resources. The Phelps-Stokes Fund of New York gave grants some years ago that have provided about the only outside support they have had. They have succeeded despite the especially unfavorable state-and-church combination found in the Portuguese territory where they work. Here is ample proof that they have used a concept and a method likely to be viable in African society even in the face of some external hostility.

Another experiment is in progress about 3,500 miles north and west of Kambini, at Asaba, Nigeria. Kenneth H. Prior, member of the United Church of Canada, for twelve years an agricultural missionary in Angola (Portuguese West Africa), in 1938 went to Nigeria under the Church Missionary Society (Anglican). Nigerian agriculture was at its lowest ebb in this generation. A five-gallon tin of palm oil for export brought nine pence instead of the ten shillings paid during World War I. Much cultivable land had been abandoned. The quick-growing tropical forest was advancing. Tens of thousands were leaving the rural communities in desperation, seeking the barest living at jobs of any sort on the rivers, along the coast, and in the urban centers. It seemed a tough time to begin an experiment in comprehensive rural Christian community development.

Kenneth Prior spent four years in feeling his way, by inaugurating tentative teaching projects, getting to know the Africans' views and life patterns, drawing in the interests of the Scotch Presbyterian and British Methodist missions, talking with government, and creating a plan.

Where was enough suitable land to be found? Nigeria is the most populous single colony left in the world. Twenty-four million people live on 338,500 square miles. Much of the land in the north is the hot sand on the edge of the Sahara, and in the south are heavy delta swamps. The over-all figure of seventy-one persons per square mile does not reflect the density of the better farming sections, nor the city of Ibadan with its population of 335,000. Good land was hard to get.

Then one day Mr. Prior was asked to speak on "Improved Agriculture" to the Asaba Farmers' Cooperative Union. About twenty came. When questions were in order the chairman said, "We understand you are looking for land for a farm school. What do you want?"

Mr. Prior said, "A large area, preferably on the banks of the

[48]

Niger River, with a stream running through it, a falls in the stream if possible, a portion of the land flooded at high water, some swamp, some good arable land, some bush, an elevation for building, a clay deposit, a rock deposit, and on, or near, a road." He reckoned he had them stumped completely. The chairman quietly replied, "We think we can meet all those requirements. Will you come and see the land?"

Three days later after miles and miles of bush-path tramping, Mr. Prior met the Farmers' Cooperative Union again. He described a site that had just about everything except the falls and said it would do.

"How much do you want?" asked the chairman.

"About five square miles," replied Prior.

"You may have it," they said. "When will you mark it out?"

The story of this meeting is significant in four ways. It shows the active desire for helpful change; the power of decision of an African rural group; the confidence in the Christian missionary and missions; and the overcoming of an ancient and powerful tradition against ceding land to outsiders in order to gain a new, desirable end.

The Asaba Rural Training and Demonstration Center is supported by the three missions named, by the Nigerian Government, and by the British Colonial Office in London. It has received some aid from the Carnegie Corporation of New York.

Its program design and training courses have considerable resemblance to Kambini's. It works with Africans for inclusive Christian development of the whole of life. It works intensively at instruction, demonstration, and experiment on the land at Asaba. Major efforts are also made to expand and extend the work to all reachable communities. The whole undertaking is Christian-sponsored, and all available forces and channels of the

[49]

Christian church are utilized in realizing its aims. The work in all its phases is freely open to all the members of the community —animists, Moslems, Roman Catholics, or others.

Asaba has at least one external advantage not enjoyed at Kambini. It is cordially and strongly supported by government. As a matter of fact, it has received some assurances of government financial support over its first ten-year period of about $500,000. This is one of the two largest sums ever promised by government to a Protestant enterprise in Africa. It should permit Asaba, with the right personnel, a fairly prompt material development.

Two observations might be made, however, and not only about Asaba and Kambini. First, the church has done some of its best work through the centuries in meeting the combined spiritual-temporal need of human society when it was least favored by current government. Second, material development in building inclusive Christian community is evermore secondary to spiritual development. Fundamentally, it is the spirit alone that can conceive, determine, and assure a Christian community capable of including all the people and all the life of all the people.

Chapter Three

WIDENING EDUCATIONAL NEEDS

NEARLY EVERYWHERE IT HAS GONE IN THE WORLD, PROTESTANTISM has laid a great emphasis on education. Many of the great schools of North America originally were institutions created by the Protestant churches and their clergy and laity. While the whole structure of Roman Catholicism rests on unquestioning obedience to the infallible church, Protestantism teaches that man's guide for his faith and conduct are God's Holy Word and his indwelling Spirit. The foundations of Protestant faith, therefore, are an alert conscience and an understanding of the Scriptures. Furthermore, these two are the very dynamic of Protestantism, for it is the responsibility of every Christian every day to grow in a more discerning conscience and a deeper understanding of God's will for men as revealed in his Word. While in Roman Catholicism, perhaps especially among the laity, education aims at making the Christian more obedient to the teachings of the church, in Protestantism it seeks to enlighten him. In the former the burden of responsibility rests on the church; in the latter, upon the individual.

We see, then, that in the Protestant view of life, education is

[51]

absolutely essential, and this is true everywhere—in Europe, America, Asia, and Africa.

On one hand, in Africa, the purpose of education is to develop the personality, enlighten the conscience, strengthen the character of the African; thus education gives aid toward the salvation and the perfecting of the whole man. On the other hand, its aim is to bring to the people the Word of God, which is God's rule of faith and conduct; thus education is a means of evangelism.

In China, Japan, Latin America, or some other parts of the world, the Christian missions, because they work among advanced people with their own culture and discipline of the mind, might perhaps seek to fulfill their task without sponsoring an elaborate program of formal education. But in many parts of Africa people live in such a primitive stage that a wide education is essential in order to make the message of the gospel accessible.

In North America, the education of a man grows out of the total impact on his personality of family, church, society, and school. In Africa, in a primitive and animistic environment, the family and society have less in this line to offer the individual. The church does not yet have the strength nor the facilities it does in North America. Thus in Africa, the Christian school is the primary institution capable of lifting up youth.

It must be said that all the Protestant missions working in Africa do not agree on the extent nor the amount of education necessary to achieve the purpose. There are those who believe that a broad educational policy is necessary to give to the Christian message its full interpretation. There are others who fear that too large a program may divert effort from the essential task, which is to proclaim the message of salvation. This brings up an all-important question: whether the Christian message is for the soul alone or whether it aims at redeeming and uplifting the whole personality of man. It is to be remembered that Jesus not only preached, but taught and healed, and, as the Good Shepherd, wanted his sheep to have abundant life.

If education is to achieve its good goal in Africa, it must help destroy superstitious beliefs in ancestral spirits, magic, and witchcraft. But destroying these beliefs without replacing them by other and better ones will do only harm to Africa. This is where the great responsibility of missions toward education lies. Governments in their lay schools can help destroy vain beliefs, but they have little new faith to contribute. Christian education is the kind that can best contribute spiritually constructive concepts. This is so true that an official British document about education says: "It is work which we think can only be done by men and women who are sincere, convinced, and practicing Christians, and it is in fact settled policy that the education we are to offer the Africans shall be Christian education." [1]

Thousands of Africans want education more than anything else, even more than immediate wealth. Someone has said Africans are "education-mad." Many of them see their poor condition compared to that of the rest of the world and think that education in itself will remedy this situation. Even in their ignorance and poverty they know, with Sir Francis Bacon, that "knowledge is power." Experience has shown us clearly that education does not cure all ills. But education is an aid that Christian missions in Africa cannot overlook.

The best among the governments and industrial groups in Africa are directly interested in encouraging education. They require, for one thing, an educated body of men and women to supply their need for technical and professional workers.

---

[1] *Colony and Protectorate of Kenya Special Recruitment for African Education,* p. 8. Published by Government of Kenya, September, 1950.

Africans are often very critical of the governments and the missions for not giving them all the education they want. An African newspaper in a leading article said: "If Africans are ignorant, it is because Europeans have not given them education." [1] At the core of this statement is the fact that at this stage Africans can do comparatively little to teach themselves, and if there is to be education, it must be done by missions, governments, and industry. Nearly all governments in Africa, both colonial and free, have been slow to respond to this demand for education. To some of them the problems of money and qualified personnel have been real difficulties. Others have simply not wanted Africans educated. It has been Protestant missions almost everywhere that pioneered in African education.

Roman Catholics have oftentimes preceded and exceeded the Protestants in the good training of their own clergy. They still do in a number of places. But Roman Catholics have in few if any cases been the first and strongest leaders in moves for the education of the mass of the people. They are now doing their best work in this aspect of education where they have been stimulated or even forced to do it by the public opinion chiefly created by Protestant education and where they have had access to government funds to pay the bills. Their income and its sources and their expenditures for mission and other work are not generally published as are Protestant figures, so one cannot speak with full assurance concerning them. They are generally believed to receive a good deal of "hidden" money given by certain governments and industry but not made publicly known by the donors. It is an impression gained from government and Roman Catholic lay sources that over the years Roman Catholic missions have probably spent on general education in Africa a much smaller

[1] *Ibid.,* p. 7.

[54]

proportion of their own church-given funds than have Protestant missions.

Even Protestant and Roman Catholic missions together have at their disposal a very limited personnel and supply of funds. They cannot alone do the whole job of public education. Probably most Protestants believe that they should not, even if they could. The people, through their governments, should have the chief responsibility. However, the occasional African accusation that missions are willing to give an elementary education to make the Africans useful to them, but no more, so that white supremacy will be protected, is generally unfounded so far as Protestant missions are concerned.

The answer of governments when such criticisms are made of them by Africans is that progress cannot be one sided; educational progress, social, political, and economic are all related. Without money, there can be no schools; without economic development, there can be no money; without skilled artisans and other trained personnel there can be no economic development; without schools there can be no artisans and trained personnel. Without the wealth produced by the natural resources of Africa, the cost of education and other social expansion cannot be met. There is a close mathematical relation between the social services and the capacity of a country to pay their cost. An African answer to this is that Africans are not getting a just share of the wealth already being produced in their area, and that they are unwilling to go on helping to produce more and more for foreigners.

The Christian church is heavily involved in all this. Three facts have special significance for the future in this matter of education. (1) Education of the laity in practically every part of Africa south of the Sahara has been pioneered by Protestant missions. (2) As the influence of this education has grown and as all but a few governments have gradually assumed more relation and financial aid to education, the Roman Catholic missions have greatly increased their program of lay education in most areas, largely on government funds, and have sought wherever possible (in some cases successfully) to obtain a monopoly of public aid for their schools. (3) The Christian church and mission in Africa still carry perhaps 85 per cent of the educational load south of the Sahara, measured in number of pupils, but governments are almost certain in the coming decade to assume more and more responsibility, as they should. The problems of state-church relationships will then grow, with possible further divergencies between Protestant and Roman Catholic views and actions.

In the meantime, the Roman Catholics have, within a rather few years, seemed to realize the tremendous opportunity they were missing in public education; they have now gained in some areas much of what it took a couple of generations for the Protestants to build. Today in most parts of Africa there is keen competition between Roman Catholic and Protestant schools, for both groups well know that he who holds youth today will greatly influence the church tomorrow.

DIVERSITY IN EDUCATIONAL PATTERNS

When we try to understand African educational problems, policies, and achievements—and the same can be said about anything concerning Africa—we must never forget that diversity is a vital factor. There is nothing simple nor uniform about the situation in Africa. There is scarcely one single statement that can be made that would apply to the whole of Africa. There are more than eight hundred different African languages. Every ruling power and every self-governing country has its own cultural background, language, and system of education.

Widening Educational Needs

The educational policies in the dependent territories follow very closely the general colonial policies. France's colonial policies as enunciated during World War II will help to illustrate this point. Early in 1944, the French held a conference at Brazzaville and drew up recommendations on political, economic, and social development. In the preamble of these recommendations is this sentence: "The goals of the work of civilization being accomplished by France in her colonies does away with any idea of autonomy and all possibility of evolution outside the unit of the French Empire; the constitution of self-government, however far away in prospect, is not to be considered." [1]

French colonies are parts of greater France, and are not treated as separate units that may become self-governing and self-sufficient. The policy envisages the assimilation of peoples of different cultures into French civilization. French spirit and culture seek to permeate everything.

Let us see how this policy of assimilation applies to French educational principles.

If there is to be one empire and one culture, there must also be one language: French. There is no room for the African vernacular languages in official schools. Mission schools alone use them. Most of the missions require two years of vernacular school before entrance into French-language schools. While government in French areas is working toward setting up its own school system, important subsidies have been granted to mission schools, particularly to those of French origin.

Britain, on the other hand, has a policy of leading every dependent territory to self-government within the commonwealth. Every territory has some chance of keeping much of its own per-

[1] Translated from *La Conférence Africaine Française-Brazzaville*, p. 35. Alger, Commissariat aux Colonies, 1944.

[57]

sonality and physiognomy, its culture and language. Applied to education, this policy means that each country can more or less work out its own aims and programs and preserve and develop its own culture, with such assimilations as it desires. This general policy, however, is subjected to some severe strains in certain East and Central African British areas where strong and aggressive white and Indian resident communities are determined to play a leading role in the future of the territories in which they live.

The various British colonial governments are all aware of their responsibility toward the Africans. In primary, elementary, and to some extent in secondary education, they have partially met this responsibility by granting substantial subsidies to all mission schools, regardless of national origin or creed.

In the Belgian Congo, the government has few schools of its own. Under Roman Catholic political pressures in Belgium, it has sought to hand its Congo educational responsibility over to Roman Catholic missions. There are few countries in the world where government has allowed itself to be more completely identified educationally with the Roman Catholic Church than in Congo. This has happened in spite of the fact that Belgium is not officially a Roman Catholic country and within its own borders has fought for and maintained a system of "free" (*i. e.*, nonclerical) education for those desiring it. Nevertheless, in Congo about 1925, the Roman Catholic Church was given a monopoly of state aid and recognition in education for a period of twenty years. This was when the Roman Catholic missions really became educationally active in Congo—forty-five years after they first entered the territory.

The principle of equal treatment of all missions in the matter of education and some related matters, regardless of creed or national origin—a principle agreed to in 1885, 1908, and 1921 in

treaties and in the Colonial Charter by successive Belgian authorities, but never lived up to—was for the first time put into law
by the Belgian parliament in 1946 during the wave of international good will that followed World War II. The Congo Government is now seeking to put this into effect.

In the Union of South Africa, mission schools are generally
subsidized.

In Portuguese and Spanish colonies, neither governments nor
the Roman Catholic Church are doing much in education, and
at the same time Protestant education is severely hampered by
government restrictions. It is no surprise that the Africans in those
areas, many of them, feel the future is bleak.

In Liberia, mission schools are welcomed but have not in the
past been subsidized. Some government grants are now being
offered, however. Certain conditions make the work very difficult,
but the future seems promising.

THE QUESTION OF SUBSIDIES

Governments subsidize mission schools because they recognize
that thus the work will be done efficiently and economically. This
arrangement is not without benefits to and from all three parties
involved. Missions put in their zeal, their knowledge of the African
mind and heart, their trained personnel; governments give their
funds, their authority, their standards; Africans present their
minds, their eager determination for self-improvement, their po-
tentialities for the future.

Although government subsidies are of financial help to missions,
they create a number of problems in the principles involved and
in their practical application.

Some American missionaries think of the unique and sharp ways
in which separation of church and state has developed in their

[59]

homeland and would refuse government subsidies. In African life there is no such thing as separation of the spiritual from the political or from any other aspect of human life. Nor is there any such separation of church and state in the cultural and political pattern of any of the six European powers ruling in Africa. Nor is there as yet any curtailment of religious content and teaching in subsidized schools.

Under these circumstances, it is a grave question whether American missions should summarily refuse subsidies in Africa solely or even principally on the ground of remaining true to the American pattern. In doing so, they might easily lay themselves open to the charge of attempting to introduce an element of American politics and of American interpretation of the Protestant principle of separation of church and state into the colonies of a foreign power.

Moreover, the Africans generally, Protestants included, are not likely to understand refusal. This is especially true in those areas where there are few or no neutral (government) schools, and where Protestants are systematically excluded from Roman Catholic schools, even from those receiving large grants from public funds. They pay their tax money; they are told this money is paid the government for school, medical, and other services that they are to get back directly and freely; the only way they, as Protestants, can get education is through Protestant mission schools. Will these now deny them, their own African children, bettered education through refusing to accept tax money the Africans themselves have paid, merely because it has passed through government hands?

But there are problems of another nature. Governments naturally want strict control and accounting of subsidies. Though one hears, rightly or wrongly, of great laxity in certain quarters in regard to keeping the proper records, Protestant educational missionaries by and large want to make all the reports and returns required. These are many, and missionaries have more and more the frustrating feeling of being mere government employees, hampered in their Christian work by increasing government regulations and bureaucratic demands.

In a progressively subsidized mission system, the African personnel can have a strong tendency to consider government and not the mission as their employer. This has created divided loyalty and disputation that is detrimental to the work.

Another difficulty is that in some territories, because of the subsidies granted, the government claims, probably rightly, that it must impose its curricula and programs. These sometimes leave too little place in regular school hours for what the missions consider central: the religious training of the child.

Further, acceptance of government educational subsidies for the training of school teachers, clerks, medical and nursing personnel, agricultural and trade workers, technicians, and skilled men and women of all kinds, *except ministers,* could in the long run—and not very long, at that—produce trained laymen far more advanced and capable in their fields than the clergy are in theirs. With what result? Christian ministers would lose touch with the young and vigorous leaders of all the other phases of life, and one more ditch would have been dug in this new African life between the spiritual and the secular. The ditch could become a chasm, where scarcely a line existed before.

If subsidies are to be accepted for what in the West is called "secular" education, let the Protestant missions everywhere get comparable funds of their own, and personnel and equipment, for the best possible training of the Christian ministry. For without such ministry seconded by such laity, with the bonds of Christ's love drawing them together and drawing all men to himself, Africa will not become Christian; the inclusive, spirit-controlled Christian community will not be reality in Africa.

Despite the efforts of governments, missions, and certain industrial enterprises such as the Firestone rubber interests in Liberia and the Union Minière copper people in Congo, there are still millions of African children who have never had an opportunity to receive even the rudiments of an education. There is no place in Africa where universal compulsory education exists. Perhaps it never will exist within this generation. The South African Government claims it spends more per capita on the education of its native population than any other country in Africa. Of course, the ultimate goal in Africa is that every child shall eventually have a place in a classroom under a qualified teacher.

The aim of education is to bring the whole community into fuller life. The aim of the teacher is not to teach some subjects to some children of the community, but rather to approach the whole community from an educational angle. This interpretation of education has been especially successful in East Africa, where the Jeanes System, first devised for the rural communities of the southern United States, has been adapted and applied.

PROBLEMS AND OPPORTUNITIES

One of the most discussed problems in African education is the place of the vernacular. Some of the more than eight hundred African languages are spoken by fewer than one thousand people. It is obvious that schools cannot be conducted in all these languages with the necessary textbooks and qualified teachers. In any event, the vernacular can be the medium for only a few years. The African languages are very rich in expressing all phases of African life, but they are limited in a vast range of things now outside the knowledge and experience of those who speak them. One can readily see that it is impossible to teach world geography or modern science in the African languages.

If education is to produce its best, it must use, along with the vernacular, a European language. Africans readily accept this fact and enthusiastically engage in language study. As a rule they show a gift for it and learn very quickly. Thousands of Africans every year pass academic and other examinations in languages foreign to them, a feat that relatively few students in our countries are prepared to undertake.

The education of girls is a special problem because of its significance and difficulties. It is impossible to achieve a better society without raising the level of the family. An intelligent, educated woman makes a better wife and mother, and creates a better home. But the difficulties are considerable.

Most important is the conservatism of the parents—"a woman is an inferior being without brains"—and the girls' resignation to this attitude. In African society the wife is a kind of servant. The more educated she is, the less blindly obedient she is to her husband. It is a tragedy that often educated girls have great difficulty finding husbands. So the economic factor enters in; parents fear to lose the dowry that suitable marriage brings for all African girls. Above everything, the African girl is *the* guarantee of the life continuity of the tribe; that is not to be trifled with by any newfangled education.

Another difficulty is the usual degree of inactivity of missions in this matter. The education of girls is more expensive per capita if it is of the proper type, which is training for motherhood and married life, and it requires much more patience than that of boys. Numbers of missionaries, including single women prepared especially for work among girls and women, have in the past gradually

[63]

shifted to work with boys and young men. There are always more of the latter than can be accommodated, eager and quick to learn, responsive and appreciative. So the girls too often are neglected.

It is important to give the best available education to a selected group of prospective leaders who will take responsibilities in their own Christian and surrounding communities as pastors, teachers, physicians, nurses, agriculturists, or in any other kind of work. Most of the missions have developed some theological, educational, and medical training courses to prepare Africans for badly-needed service in their own mission institutions. But because of these immediate, pressing demands, very few missions have carried out plans to train educated men and women to exemplify Christian belief and living in government offices, in business, or in the different trades. Sometimes educated men who have gone into such services have been accounted as "lost" to the missions.

The British colonies in West Africa since World War II have begun the development of two university colleges. Probably many readers have heard of Achimota in the Gold Coast. Its vice-principal and one of its outstanding teachers was Kwegyir Aggrey. Ibadan in Nigeria is not so well known. For all East African territories, there is one university college at Makerere. In the Union of South Africa, education of college level is given to Africans at Fort Hare. All these are government sponsored. Lovedale and Adams College in South Africa are excellent mission-sponsored schools. So is Fourah Bay in Sierra Leone, which is now, however, being taken over for still higher education.

In French territories each capital has a good secondary school. Dakar, in French West Africa, has a medical school for students from all the French African territories. French schools are open to all, regardless of race. In French territories the Cameroun Christian College is the only mission-sponsored secondary school.

[64]

In the Belgian Congo, Protestant union schools at Kimpese and Bolenge are pioneers in the higher education of teachers and pastors. Mission schools in the Kasai and the Katanga are increasing and raising their levels. At Kimpese a union medical training institution is being built, with government and Belgian philanthropic foundation aid. This is the first large subsidized union venture for Protestants in Congo.

In Liberia the College of West Africa and the newly located Cuttington College are mission supported. Liberia College, a government school, is to be the nucleus of a university. Booker Washington Agricultural and Industrial Institute, begun by American missions and philanthropic organizations, is scheduled to become a unit in the new university.

In Portuguese, Spanish, and Italian colonies there is little progress toward higher education. It would seem that Protestant missions need to assume a special responsibility here, as they generally have in primary and elementary education in these colonies.

Besides the possibilities for advanced education on the continent, hundreds of scholarships are offered for studies overseas. Eight hundred Africans (almost all from British, Liberian, and Ethiopian areas) are studying in the United States, 2,580 in Britain, and about 1,000 in France. Many of these are being educated with private funds.

In Africa at the present time education is still the privilege of a select few, so it is especially important that this tiny minority receive the sort of schooling that will lead to the development of a strong sense of responsibility and service to the community. This little minority has the tremendous opportunity of pioneering with a new sense of community in the new Africa "a-borning," guided by a religion that has done so much already for man despite man's human frailties and sins.

[65]

To do this, the minority needs in this critical time as never before the universal help of all committed Christians. It needs that help through Christian government officials, through Christian business and industrial men, through Christian philanthropic, educational, and scientific personalities at home and in Africa, through Christian men and women in North America, Britain, and France where African students are now learning much more than is in the college catalogue.

If war, peace, trade, and communication are global, so, too, is education. It cannot be done solely in an African bush school or a Christian institute or a university college. African education is now a process shared by all foreigners and Africans in Africa and by all people and institutions and business abroad that in any way come into contact with Africans physically, or with their minds or hearts. If Christians, African and foreign, want Christian community in Africa, all Christians everywhere need to work for it, beginning right where they are. Every Christian witness anywhere in this tight-knit world today is a Christian witness everywhere.

LITERACY AND LITERATURE

One of our aims is to reach the mass of the people through a wide program of education, even if it gives only the rudiments. One hundred and fifty years ago, the continent of Africa south of the Sahara was almost completely illiterate. Some eight hundred languages were spoken, but only one or two had been reduced to writing. Today there are at least 390 written African languages, and the peoples who speak them can have part or all of the Bible at first hand.

It was Christian missionaries who undertook the tedious task of bridging the gap between speech and writing, who in infinite patience listened to the Africans speak, made notes, gradually established a vocabulary and an orthography, and translated the Word into the languages of the people.

LITERACY

There is still a high percentage of illiteracy in Africa. However, local conditions and world events have brought a new awareness of the need for literacy; and simple methods, again devised by painstaking, observing missionaries, have made learning much easier.

There are also new incentives to learn. Men went away to war; they learned to read and write in the army. They wished to write home to their families. If only their families could read! People went to work in distant mines; the old ties would be broken unless they could communicate with the home folks. The farmer saw that he could learn better methods if he could read. The villager who was overcharged at the market because he could not read had the incentive to learn. And when a "literacy campaign" came to his village he saw men and women no younger than he, no smarter than he, learning the secrets of the "talking leaf."

Illustrative of the way, by trial and error, literacy workers have found suitable methods, is the Mindolo experiment carried on by Mrs. Hope Hay, a missionary in Northern Rhodesia.[1]

In this country adult education was confined to night schools in the cities and to classes held by churches in preparation for church membership. Probably three-quarters of the adult population was illiterate.

The United Missions in the Copper Belt has a mission station at Mindolo bordering on one of the African mine compounds. Here in 1943, Mrs. Hay held an unofficial African Women's Insti-

---

[1] *Northern Rhodesia Learns to Read.* Education Overseas 1. London, Edinburgh Press House, 1947.

tute. Faced with the fact that the ordinary school textbooks were not suitable in content for these grown women, nor the usual classroom techniques applicable, Mrs. Hay worked out her own system of lessons, based on whole words and sentences. These were drawn on large sheets of paper and crudely illustrated. They were used only at Mindolo, and only by women.

In 1943, the Colonial Office in London published a paper on "Mass Education in African Society." When the paper was reviewed in Rhodesia, the government, mine management, and mission groups decided to tackle the problem of adult illiteracy together. In 1945, work was started in the Mindolo mine compound, the government financing the experiment. Mrs. Hay was asked to direct the work. Two experienced Jeanes supervisors were sent to assist her. Mrs. Hay gave them advance training in her own sitting room.

The experimental lessons previously worked out for the African Women's Institute formed the basis of the necessary primers, but now they were illustrated and printed. Tribal representatives in the compound were called together and the plans explained to them. One of them said, "You have come to give us sight. We people are as the blind. How can we walk forward without sight?"

Between April and the end of May, there were sixty new literates, and by the end of July, there were 193. Over twenty had already taught one or more friends. All could read their own vernacular newspaper, and they could now write to their families and friends. The average time it took a student to learn was three weeks. Some Africans called it magic, others a miracle.

Describing how to overcome the diffidence of the older student, one supervisor said of his approach, "When a man says he cannot read and write, you simply say to him, 'My dear friend, you can read. Do you not see and read the spoor of animals on the ground?'

You give some more examples of the things that he sees in his daily life. Then you say, 'Do you know the difference between the marks of a wild pig and of a lion? Then you will be able to read the marks on the paper, too. You will see how very quickly the new power comes.' "

The Mindolo experiment was so successful that training was offered for full-time literacy supervisors and for volunteers giving part-time service. During that first year twenty-three full-time and forty-five part-time workers were trained. They were used in different localities by both mission and government agencies. Sixteen Europeans took the training course—missionaries, educational officers, principals of teacher training institutions.

Follow-up work is needed. In the Copper Belt new literates are given help if they need it in letter-writing and in keeping simple household accounts. Small groups are formed for reading and discussion. Barriers are being broken down as clerks teach miners and road menders, and detribalization is retarded by making possible contact with home.

Missionary workers in the literacy field recognize that literacy is not an end in itself, but a valued way to evangelism and Christian education. "We are finding that the Gospels are among the first books asked for by new literates," says a report from Sierra Leone, "and from several places in the chiefdoms where we have been working, there have been requests to the missions for catechists."

In 1947-48, Dr. Frank C. Laubach spent eight months on a literacy tour, working with missions and governments in West, Central, and South Africa. In the Cameroun he made charts in the two-hundredth language he has put into this form during his world experience. Literacy work was begun in thirty-five new languages on his second trip to Africa in 1950. The seminars con-

[69]

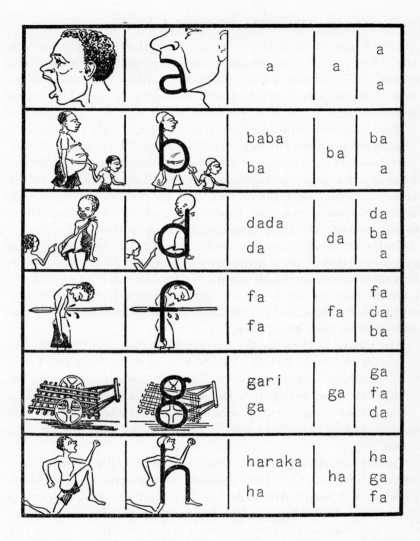

Here is the first Laubach lesson in Kiswahili. The student learns to associate names and shapes of pictures with sounds and shapes of letters.

ducted by this apostle of literacy have stimulated much interest, and presses are busy in many areas turning out primers and the two works Dr. Laubach uses as second readers, *The Story of Jesus,* a series of booklets telling in a very simple vocabulary the greatest story ever told, and *Making Everybody's World Safe,* which gives big ideas in plain style.

One result of the Laubach campaign in Portuguese East Africa is the fact that now an African Christian serves the Christian council as specialist in literacy methods. He spends his time demonstrating the Laubach method among the missions affiliated with the council. It is reported concerning him that "The care and love manifested by the teacher reveals to the non-Christians that the church and the Lord want them."

It was in Beira that an old African came to bid farewell to the literacy team, saying, "We cannot find words to tell you what you have done for us. We feel like a dog which cannot speak, but can only wag its tail. But we will thank the Lord for you every day. May God keep you well to help the whole world as you have helped us."

LITERATURE

When a man becomes literate, he needs to have something to read; literature follows literacy as naturally as B follows A. In theory, that is. To produce suitable literature, and in sufficient quantities and different languages, is not easy in Africa. But here, too, the missionaries have pioneered. There are literature departments in several Christian councils. In British territories, the colonial governments are giving valuable assistance.

The African Literature Committee of Northern Rhodesia has developed some thirty titles, on such topics as tribal history, folklore, home management, child care, and African customs. Some are of African authorship. There are over 130 titles in the African Home Library, little booklets published in simple English by the International Committee on Christian Literature for Africa, on topics within the people's range of interest and sold at a price they can afford to pay.

Two groups in the United States and Canada are particularly concerned with literature for Africa. One is the Committee on World Literacy and Christian Literature, of which Dr. Laubach is special consultant and representative on the field. The other is the Africa Committee, which has in its purview all African concerns and serves as the North American Section of the International Committee on Christian Literature for Africa.[1]

This latter committee, which has its principal office in London, is unique in its composition and sweep. It was formed in 1929 to "promote the production, publication, and distribution of literature for use in connection with missionary work in Africa."

In addition to publishing the African Home Library, mentioned earlier, the International Committee publishes *Listen: News from Far and Near,* a periodical for the African village home. Periodical literature is essential to encourage the new literate to read; he keeps up his reading, and his neighbors see him receive the journal from time to time, which is in itself a satisfaction. The more advanced reader can contribute to it, participate in its contests, solve the Bible puzzles.

The quarterly bulletin of the International Committee, *Books for Africa,* aims to serve those working in Africa who need information on books relating to that continent and news of literature plans in different areas.

---

[1] Both are committees of the Division of Foreign Missions of the National Council of the Churches of Christ in the U. S. A.

PRODUCTION

Books presuppose presses. Missions have been in the van here, too. As early as 1829 the first missionary press arrived at Morija, Basutoland. It was a wooden press, and a supply of type, paper, and ink came with it. Twenty years later, the four Gospels and the book of *Acts* had been printed. By 1920, there were twelve African workers on the staff; now there are some eighty. In one year, the Morija Press has printed 380,000 books of sixty-two titles and 103,000 copies of periodicals in several languages. The newspaper printed at Morija in 1863 was probably the first paper for Africans to be regularly issued in southern Africa.

Another very old institution is the Lovedale Press, at Lovedale, South Africa. A missionary who arrived in 1823 brought with him a small press, type, paper, and ink. Three days after the press had been set up, fifty copies of the Xhosa alphabet had been run off. The next year a speller and first reader were ready, and two years later a grammar. The entire Bible was available in Xhosa by 1857.

A magazine in English and Xhosa, *Indaba* (The News) began to appear in 1862. Lovedale Press showed its faith in the capacity of the native African very early: in 1876, all three editors of *Isigidimi* (The Christian Messenger) were Bantu. Today the Lovedale Press prints books and other materials in ten languages.

La Librarie Evangélique au Congo (LECO), at Léopoldville, Belgian Congo, a union press and bookshop, is the largest financial undertaking under any Christian council in Africa. It was set up in 1935 as a central Bible depot and bookshop to serve all the missions in Congo.

By June, 1950, LECO had produced 25,400,000 pages in books, pamphlets, and periodicals, in English, French, Portuguese, and seven African languages. There are now hymnals, primers, readers, periodicals, and adult literacy materials.

[73]

Dr. George W. Carpenter, the managing director, writes, "The demand for Christian literature and for schoolbooks is completely without precedent here. I had to place two orders with one Belgian firm in one day, as the quantity of one particular book I thought sufficient for several months was completely spoken for in orders received during the day. The British and Foreign Bible Society put in hand ten thousand Kikongo Bibles, planning to bind five thousand now and hold the remainder in sheets till needed. I have already transmitted to the society three separate orders for five thousand each, and have other smaller orders in hand. The first five thousand will have to be portioned out in driblets to the many mission stations requiring them, and will sell out in a day. Even the Bible school at Kingoyi has no Bibles for its students. A few years ago, we used to print from four to five thousand Lingala hymnals every three years or so. Now we have an edition of fifteen thousand on press, and it will probably not last more than a year."

In many British territories a good deal of the initiative for the preparation of wholesome books for general reading is in the hands of government or government-aided organizations. The pioneer work of the missionaries in the literature field is recognized by government publication bureaus, and missionaries have in many cases been appointed to assist them.

The report of the East African Literature Bureau [1] gives an idea of their scope. This bureau aims at the "publication of books and pamphlets to stimulate thought; books for the education of adult and child; assistance to indigenous authors; the development of periodical literature; and the building up of library service." The report says, "In all these fields, some work has been done to meet the need, by missions, commercial publishers, and government offices, but there was no attempt to attack the problem as a whole,

[1] *East Africa High Command.* East Africa Literature Bureau, 1949.

and none of the agencies had staff to devote to any particular problem for an adequate length of time. The mission bookshops in the three territories—the pioneers in this development—have been of great service and have given the bureau every support."

DISTRIBUTION

Production is effective only as it is followed up by distribution. Books on the shelves are sterile. This matter of moving books off the shelves is a general problem; in Africa, difficulties of communication and of transportation add to it. There should be bookshops and literature distribution centers at all the main mission stations. Libraries are needed; in British territories the Carnegie Corporation and the British Council have given help toward this end. There are attempts to put books where Africans will see them, to sell them at book stalls in the native markets, to place them where readers will buy them when they buy cloth or other commodities. Colporteurs are badly needed, for much of the distribution must be through mobile units. A bookmobile is being used successfully in South Africa, in the Lovedale Colportage Caravan scheme.

BY AFRICANS FOR AFRICANS

In March, 1951, there appeared in Cape Town, South Africa, the first issue of *The African Drum*. The subtitle reads, "A Magazine of Africa for Africa." "In that phrase," says an editorial, "we recognize the existence of more than 150 million Bantu and Negro inhabitants of this continent, whom we will attempt to reach for the first time in history with words that will express their thoughts, their impulses, their endeavors, and ultimately their souls."

The magazine, which is in large format and profusely illustrated, reprinted *Cry, the Beloved Country* serially, and main-

[75]

tains departments on music, art, folklore, sports, fashions, religion, and readers' views. It says categorically, "This paper will be 100 per cent African."

The missionary forces have realized increasingly the necessity of indigenous authorship, whenever and wherever it is possible. Indeed, Africans are needed at every point of the literacy-literature program. When there are translations to be made or original writing to be created, they themselves have the figures of speech, the turn of phrase, the medium of expression that makes the words and ideas authentic. African artists should illustrate the books, Africans print and sell them, trained African librarians put them into the hands of the African reading public.

It is in this direction that missions have moved, though with what often seems unnecessary slowness. The number of African writers is increasing. The contests held by the International African Institute (London) have proved stimulating. The Margaret Wrong Memorial Fund offers prizes for manuscripts by Africans. Governments and missions have given scholarships enabling African students to attend the School of Oriental and African Studies in London and the Institute of Education, to gain skill in increasing the supply of materials in African languages. Mr. Green Richard Katongole, the first African from Uganda, East Africa, to receive a Fulbright traveling fellowship, is studying at the School of Journalism, Syracuse University. He expects on his return to edit a biweekly Christian journal and to collect and publish African stories and poems.

There is a growing African native press, serving a population increasingly literate and hungry for reading matter. Some periodicals are in English, which has become a *lingua franca* among the literate Africans in British areas, a few in vernaculars that are widely spoken, like Swahili and Hausa, and even some in vernaculars used by comparatively few. Some carry materials in several tongues; there is one in Zanzibar in which English, Arabic, and Swahili appear on the same page.

It is hard to make a paper pay on a small circulation, and most of these have only a few thousand subscribers. Each paper may be read aloud to five or ten listeners, but that does not help financially. Most newspaper offices struggle along with antiquated presses and incomplete fonts of type. Comparatively few of the employees have been trained either in journalism, printing, business management, or financial accounting.

Where European private enterprises get out papers for Africans, there is more capital and better equipment, and the circulation is from thirty thousand up. The *East African Standard* issues a paper in Swahili, and the *London Daily Mirror* sponsors two in English. In purely African enterprises, Zik Press in Lagos, Nigeria, is outstanding; its *West African Pilot* has a circulation of fifteen thousand, and uses a modern rotary press.

John Ross, the agent of the Glasgow Missionary Society who brought the first press to Cape Province from Great Britain, wrote in 1860, "The church should not forget that her commission extends to the world of readers, who become the men of action, for evil as much as for good." An old African expressed the same idea in positive form when he said, "Men can use fire and axes and knives against one another, but they have learned to use these things for the common good and for helping themselves to live. So may it be with these new gifts of reading and writing."

It is important that these "gifts of reading and writing" should come from Christian hands.

Dr. Maurice J. Hohlfeld, a literacy expert who visited Africa in 1950, reported, "Perhaps the most frequently repeated phrase on the lips of missionaries and natives in relationship to literacy and

[77]

literature is 'not enough.' There are not enough teachers, not enough literacy workers, not enough writers, not enough books, not enough paper, not enough printed material, not enough reading matter, not enough of everything that is necessary to proclaim the good news of the gospel of Jesus Christ. It is not too late, and yet it may be later than we think. If we do not teach the people to read, others eventually will, and they will likewise supply the type of reading matter that will win the victory for them. The pen is still mightier than the sword, and the typewriter more effective than the machine gun. Africa is anxious to learn how to read. It wants to read the good books, the Christian literature that has done so much for others. It wants to read the Book of Books for itself, and in its own language. Indeed, St. Paul might have added another phrase in his message to the Romans by saying, 'And how shall they read unless they be taught?' "

Chapter Four

COMMUNISM VERSUS CHRISTIAN COMMUNITY

THE THREE POWERFUL ORGANIZED FORCES NOW STRUGGLING FOR the minds and hearts of men in Africa can be clearly named. They are animist communalism, Stalinist communism, and Christian community.

They have a common quality, reflected in the three nouns. These all come from the root of "common," from the Latin of *communis* (*com* and *munis:* ready to be of service). They all profess that readiness.

But the dynamic quality in each of these three names, the thing that triggers them out of readiness and into action, that powers the action, that identifies and distinguishes each of the three forces and sets them one over against the other, is to be found in the three governing words: animist, Stalinist, Christian. There are many Smiths in the world, with a common heritage. But the power and direction and spiritual depth of Albert and Seth and Clement can be very different.

In Africa, in today's world, the old and classical acceptance of practical identity between communalism and communism must be challenged. For Africa refutes Webster's 1922 dictionary, which says that communalism is "substantially the same as communism." Today the word "communism," as commonly used, means Stalinist communism or some form closely related to it. Using the word in that sense we can say that although Africa is certainly communalist, it is not communist. It need never become communist, unless —but let that come a bit later.

Africa is truly and wholeheartedly communalist in its traditional way of life. It has communal ownership of land within (but not usually among) the diverse tribal groups. Its barter economy, which includes the manufacture of articles by hand, has full communal control. All of its social affairs are communally managed. Its education is almost completely communal. So are its recreation and its political organization. But through all this communalism, there is recognition of a higher being, or beings, distant but accepted. There is a God, known from afar and recognized in his power. There is religion, animism. And that spiritual belief, primitive and inadequate as it is, is the most powerful single control of this whole communal organism.

African animistic communalism has, like all social systems, its weaknesses and its strengths. It is full of superstitions. It has within it oppression and terrorism. Like all systems, it has to attempt more than it knows how to do well. In it the individual has small freedom. But at least there has been a solidarity that has enabled man to exist. In Africa's new world, it is wholly inadequate, this communalism. But it seems to have none of the features of Stalinist communism that hundreds of millions of men and women are coming to loathe, fear, hate, and increasingly to fight in today's world. Not the least of the differences—indeed the most basic of them all—is that religion really rules African communalism, whereas Stalinist communism seeks everywhere to rule religion, if not to rout and destroy it.

[80]

Communism Versus Christian Community

This basic difference between animist communalism and Stalinist communism with respect to religion is a potent factor in the Christian-communist conflict in Africa. Communalism and communism are, it is true, social systems with certain root likenesses. It could seem logical to expect that communalism, since it is now forced into major changes by outside world pressures, might find communism congenial. But two powerful factors, both in the realm of religion, favor Christianity against communism in Africa's new society now forming.

The first is that the best features of both communalism and communism are to be found in Biblical Palestinian Christianity, with very much more besides. On the other hand, their terrors and hates have no place in such Christianity. Palestinian Christianity has a special appeal to many Africans as a saving fulfillment of the best promises glimpsed in animism.

The second and what could be the deciding factor is that the communalism of African society is almost completely controlled by its religion, animism, a very imperfect revelation of God. Communism, on the contrary, rejects the spiritual idea of God and seeks to control or destroy religion among its subjects.

The African believes in the existence of God, and, more than most Western Christians, he believes in and practices the control of society by powers of the spirit, by religion. As a result, during the past century in Africa south of the Sahara, the Christian religion has won the allegiance of more Africans than any other element entering from abroad. There are more professing Christians than there are "educated" Africans or than there are Africans in industry, science, politics, or the armed forces. There are more Christians in Africa (some 21 million) south of the Sahara than the number (about 20 million) in all the rest of the so-called non-Christian world put together.

[81]

Christianity is the greatest force that has entered Africa in the past century. This truth can be demonstrated not only by numbers—numbers alone in human affairs are seldom a realist's measure of power—but more especially by what it has accomplished in Africa and what it has stimulated others to accomplish in education, literacy, literature, family life, medicine, public health, agriculture, rural community, technical training, experimental and pilot projects of wide variety; in travel, study, and observation abroad for Africans; and in other ways. All these are in addition to, although because of, the tremendous power Christianity has in winning the souls of men.

It is this predominant power, demonstrated and communicated by Christianity in the past century in the essentially fertile soil of African society, that underlies the uncompleted sentence near the beginning of this chapter: Africa need never become communist, unless . . .

The complete sentence is probably the most important thing in this book. It is this: Africa need never become communist unless the individual and group acts of yourself and myself, of millions of Christians in North America, Europe, and Africa, fall so grievously short of being really Christian, that the African, embittered at these failures and hopeless of "white man's" Christianity, turns in desperation to communism. This would be to go completely against African tradition and belief by rejecting God and by repudiating any spiritual reign over society. It would be repugnant and soul-baffling to many Africans. But it can happen.

The result would be a great blow to world Christianity, to understanding and peace, to all life as many of us in the West and in Africa know it. For it would come not principally from the hardness of heart of the Africans, but rather from our own flouting of essential Christianity in our personal and collective

[82]

acts, at home and in Africa. It would come as further, staggering proof of the Christian's failure—or perhaps man's inability—to practice Christianity in the expanding life we live.

Africans are receptive to Christianity as have been few if any other people in history. They have no closely-knit philosophy nor theology to armor their animism, as do members of most other non-Christian religions. A century's experience seems to show that Africa will become Christian if Christianity will produce what it promises. Christianity can produce only through the souls and lives of people. We are people who profess Christianity. The African looks at us. He looks at us to see what Christianity produces. What he sees is a lot of good and a lot of bad. And, partly because color enters in, he often thinks he sees more bad than good.

Color can greatly intensify perception and almost every human emotion. Color photography from a forty thousand foot elevation can reveal the earth, its heights and depths, the products of its soil and of its human inhabitants as does no other medium. Color contacts at three feet can be extremely powerful in the whole life pattern of men and women. Color in human relations often tends to highlight the bad and subdue the good. Irrational as it may be, color is nevertheless often dominant. Seen through the eyes of colored people in the world today, Christianity appears far from producing what it promises.

In such a situation, communism has a big advantage today over Christianity. For communism needs currently only to promise in Africa. At present it does nothing else. It has yet no visible productive power there. It has no chance nor challenge yet to produce in Africa. Africans have almost no way of knowing how well or poorly it produces what it promises within communist-controlled countries. Our own knowledge of this is inadequate. The African's is practically nil.

The communist promises for Africa materially, politically, and socially seem good, attractive to many in Africa as to many in other lands. The promise of complete freedom as regards color is particularly appealing. Probably many Africans feel that they would be willing to undergo many other disadvantages if only color discrimination were removed. Thus the communist promise of its removal is powerfully attractive to many Africans. Communism's essential denial of God and of any spiritual control of life is almost unknown to Africans. The eye cannot always penetrate the Iron Curtain, but the ear can hear the promises from behind it.

Africa hears echoes from China and Indo-China, from Malaya, from India, from Pakistan, Iran, and the East Indies. Those echoes, mostly of the voices of people of color, are not the harsh denunciation of communsim that comes from the white West. Why? the African asks. Color colors the answer.

An alternative to both colonialism and communism is seen by Africans to be growing in those areas also, and it tends to fan the spark in many African minds. The alternative is nationalism. The move toward nationalism is not entering Africa from without, nor is it organized. It is born in the hearts of Africans themselves, as it has been in others' hearts. It is partly a result of exasperation, frustration, fear, and hate. It is partly selfish and egoistic. But it is partly, too, the human urge to try to have to the full the fullness of life, their own life.

To a good many Africans, no doubt, nationalism appeals as a way of having their own country back; of maintaining their traditional communal solidarity as tribes and expanding it to embrace other tribes; of determining their own policies free of white domination politically, economically, and spiritually.

The current developments in the Gold Coast and Nigeria, in

the Sudan, in Libya, Tunisia, the three Moroccos (French, Spanish, and Tangier), and in former Italian Somaliland all have nationalism within them. Less visibly but just as surely, a spirit of nationalism is growing elsewhere in Africa.

Communism, we can be certain, is trying to use that growing spirit of African nationalism for its own ends. Those ends would, eventually, be the end of African nationalism, but probably most Africans are not now prepared to believe that.

In African nationalism, color is an identifiable factor. Nearly all their foreign rulers are white, and it seems simple and understandable to say, in a variety of phrases, "Throw out the whites and we shall be free." The Communists, most of them white, echo those phrases and so seem to identify themselves with Africans as few other whites do.

Non-Communist whites in their anger sometimes abet Communists in the latters' attempted self-identification with Africans. They label as Communists other non-Communist whites who sincerely seek to work with and for Africans against white domination or oppression of one kind or another. This is not only wrong; it is stupid. For it seems to assure Africans that it *is* only the Communist who is really one with them. The Communists say so. The non-Communists say so. For once they agree. It must be so.

In seeking to assess communism and nationalism today in relation to Africa, we must never underestimate this matter of color and our own failures and even crimes in regard to it. We must also remember that communism has not yet been challenged to produce anything in Africa except disturbances and promises.

With Christianity it is otherwise. It must both promise and produce in Africa, for it has been there a long time. Its religious missions are many. The foreign governments in Africa are all from "Christian" countries. So are most of the industry and commerce, the new law and social structure being introduced. Christianity's promises for a century or more have been good, and it has produced a great deal of good.

However, Christianity has a range and height of promises that are incomparable in human history. The greater the promises and the hopes they raise, the greater seem any failures to produce. There are many in Africa who, grateful for the promises and the good produced, still feel the failures are greater. They may be right. But whether they are wrong or right, that is their feeling, and it largely controls their actions.

It is not only in Africa, however, that Christianity must both promise and produce if it is to win Africa. It has both to promise and produce overseas—in Western Europe and in North America, and also in the Near East and the Middle East and the Far East. It has, indeed, to produce everywhere, for it is the only global religion. An element of the inner power of global Protestant Christianity is that in its operations everywhere it is committed to operation in the open. It can erect no iron curtain. Its failures and its successes are as open as the open Bible from whence its open promises come. It has created the best developments of democracy with this policy of open operation, opposed to all totalitarianism, to all "curtains" under whatever guise—spiritual, social, economic, political. It cannot disguise nor conceal. The genius of Protestant Christianity is as open as the open Book.

This being true, the Africans, who are more and more traveling, studying, and looking out upon the world, are almost daily learning more of the promise and the product of Christianity in countries long called Christian. They are learning, too, the product of those countries' relations with non-Christian countries of the Near, Middle, and Far East.

We ourselves know that the promise is good and that the prod-

[86]

uct is mixed. The Africans are learning that, too, but they are seeing it all through a kind of color screen that we have helped to provide with our prejudice, a color screen that tends to emphasize the bad and subdue the good. Many white people also see persons and circumstances through a color screen. It tends to emphasize for them the bad in colored people and to minimize the good. Why are we surprised when Africans look at us in the same way and have the same reaction? Every Communist effort seeks to exploit that emphasis on the bad. But much more important today in Africa than this Communist effort is the hard fact that every single element of discrimination, underprivilege, official or bureaucratic ineptness or mistake, economic retardation, even judgment and personality differences between whites and Africans is viewed through this color screen that is so largely of our own making.

Thus viewed, the bad can seem at times insufferably great. For the bad in these situations appears to Africans not so clearly resulting from the problems of mass ignorance in Africa, nor the stubborn economic facts that Europeans face in Africa, nor the human frailties found in every individual of any color. Rather, it appears to them as resulting from a hypocritical white colonialist design of the "Christian" peoples of the West against the coloreds.

The very considerable good that some foreign governments have brought into Africa appears to many Africans minuscule in comparison to this exaggerated view of the bad and in relation to the unmet needs. The eventual remedy to the two-fold problem of the actual bad done to Africa and of the emotional exaggeration of that bad on account of color does not lie in Africa alone. Africa's problem, like that of all geographic areas today, is global.

The hugeness of the problem may tempt us to heave a sigh of relief and dismiss it from our minds. If a problem is global, in a globe as large and complex and baffling as ours, surely tiny I can do little about it. Nor can my community nor even my nation. We do not have any possessions in Africa. We know almost nothing, really, about Africa. We will never even see Africa. Certainly we cannot do much about it.

But we do see Africa. We see Africa in the uranium at Oak Ridge and Hanford. We see Africa in the gold at Fort Knox—which helps make possible the $500 million for one single gaseous diffusion plant at Oak Ridge to use the uranium and a $60 billion American peace-year budget aimed at preventing war. We see Africa in the tensest single racial problem that the world faces, in the Union of South Africa. We see Africa in the only natural rubber supply that the United States and Canada had in World War II. We see Africa in the huge new air bases where some thousands of our men and hundreds of millions of our dollars have freshly gone. We see Africa in cocoa and industrial diamonds and copper and half a dozen other things we daily require. We see Africa and its colonialism among the underlying sources of disagreement between ourselves and Britain, France, and Belgium, complicating and retarding our over-all agreement on the Near East, on North Atlantic Treaty Organization matters, and on economic strategic policies in various spheres. And in the intimate life of the United States, we see Africa in sixteen million citizens, the largest visible ethnic group in our nation. We see Africa in these and other matters vitally affecting us.

And Africa sees us, more and more.

It sees us Christians in Africa badly split among ourselves. It has to learn scores of names for the separate Protestant groups, and other scores for the Roman Catholic orders of priests and nuns and lay workers. It sees the rivalries and undercutting among the Catholic orders, even though externally the Roman Catholic

Church appears to be one. It sees the differences and conflicts between Protestants, even though within each of sixteen areas in Africa they are more or less linked in Christian councils.

It sees above all in this foreign Christian church the deep gulf between Protestants and Roman Catholics, this split in the very body of Christ. We know historically, at least in a general way, how this difference came about. Our concepts of divergent Protestantism and Roman Catholicism have been long formed and they seem fairly clear, inevitable, and so more or less normal. They do not seem so to the African.

To him they are for the most part an enigma, one of the queer and inexplicable mysteries the white men have brought with them. Why children of God, lovers of Jesus, believers in Christ, sons and daughters of one Father, all communing regularly in the name of their common Saviour, nearly all of them white—why people having so much in common spiritually and culturally and all claiming one name, Christian, are so split and so opposed to one another is yet an unsolved riddle to the vast majority of Africans.

When that split and opposition develop into open physical conflict, as happens too frequently on a small scale and sometimes even on a large scale in those areas where the Roman Catholic Church has a dominant position and undertakes to stop the activities of the "heretics," African society is shocked and repelled. It seems to them no way for "Christians" to act.

Some think Catholicism may perhaps have initially a stronger appeal to Africans. Its authoritative and hierarchical structure is in some ways more like the traditional African spiritual and social pattern. Its ritual, the functioning of its priests and the limited group participation in it, are appealing, for in their own primitive animism they operated somewhat similarly. The costuming and

[89]

the pageantry of the Roman Catholic Church are also attractive for much the same reason. The relics, the rosary, the medals, the little pieces of "Mary's dress" worn by hundreds of thousands of African Catholics, all these external symbols blessed by their new religious leaders are welcome, for out of their past experience they feel they understand them and can somewhat measure their value. The confessional and priestly-given absolution seem to have special value to them also in this present long and complicated transition from animism to Christianity. When the repeated temptation to fall back on unchristian actions and methods cannot be resisted, oral assurance of forgiveness for those sins can be had.

Another considerable strength possessed at this stage by the Roman Catholic Church lies in the fact that it can train, ordain, and give ecclesiastical authority commensurate with the rank to African priests and nuns with greater "safety" than Protestants can give high church office to Africans. It can even make monseigneurs and bishops (there is one Roman Catholic African bishop south of the Sahara), thus giving full African participation at each level of rank, and yet at the same time it can retain complete spiritual, temporal, financial, and disciplinary control of all African clergy and members in the foreign white hands of the higher hierarchy. Such is the advantage, at least temporarily, of a rigid and authoritarian chain of command. The Protestants have no comparable advantage and do not wish it. But today they appear in a good many African eyes as lagging behind the Roman Church in developing and giving churchly responsibilities to African leaders.

However, Roman Catholics feel they have at least one practical disadvantage as compared to Protestants in Africa—the celibacy required of African men and women who take many of their religious vows and orders. This creates many problems, and not only in Africa. Some Roman Catholic leaders feel modifications should be studied in relation to Africa.

The generally demonstrated slowness of the Roman Church in Africa, already referred to, to undertake mass literacy and education unless it is more or less pushed to do so by the example of Protestant or government forces, is a serious weakness in the Christian enterprise in Africa. One might reasonably think that, strong as the Vatican tries to be spiritually and politically against communism and knowledgeable as it is regarding the whole European scene, it would begin to wonder if there is not some relation between mass illiteracy and today's communist domination. It seems clear to others—and I have no doubt to many Roman Catholics also—that except for East Germany, now under the allied-sanctioned Soviet military occupation, the countries in which communism is either dominant or internally most feared are those in which there has been the greatest Roman Catholic or Orthodox neglect of mass literacy and education, with the consequent failure of the peoples to achieve, among other things, land reform and economic progress.

Roman Catholic lay and clerical personalities have expressed to me and have written of their fear that mass literacy and education in Africa might open wider the doors for the entry of communism. It is true that where doors are open many things can enter. But Christianity in all its fullness can carry more through open doors than any other force in human experience. Newspapers, magazines, books, and men speaking these days repeatedly say that the basic answer to communism is a spiritual answer. Christian leaders, including the highest Roman Catholics, say that this spiritual answer is the one Christ gives to men. The Roman Catholic Church holds the view that its head is the vicar of Christ on earth.

Why, then, this fear of open doors, if Christ's own gospel, his love, his re-creative, transforming, and saving power is ready to go in? World experience has seemed to be that where the doors have been opened widest and Christ's power has gone in most freely, there the battle has gone best for man and society. God progressively gives men the freedom and capacity to use the ever-new and tremendously expanding forces that pass through rightly opened doors. The real limitation is within man himself—in his mind and spirit.

Stalinist communism versus Christian community? Christian community will win in Africa if two things happen. If the doors are opened widely by literacy, education, literature, by a greatly increased exchange of visits for study, observation, counsel, and friendship, and by an increasing national and international under-standing and cooperation, the enabling step will have been taken. But the much harder and more important thing is for Christians to do their utmost to insure that through those wide-open doors the best possible examples of Christian life and action, in every phase of life's work, enter African society. This means that at all times and in all places we will act as Christians individually and collec-tively in our home relationships. It means we commit ourselves to creating and backing Christian overseas policies and actions of governments, industry, churches, educational and philanthropic institutions, and other agencies. It means that our personnel going overseas to represent us in all these things shall be persons who rightly exemplify these qualities.

With such a practical demonstration of Christian community at work in Africa, neither animist communalism nor Stalinist communism can win or hold Africa's rising people.

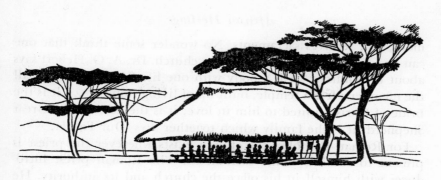

Chapter Five

FOR A STRONG, FREE CHURCH

WE BELIEVE THIS TO BE A GENERALLY ACCEPTABLE STATEMENT OF the aim of foreign missions: "The supreme and controlling aim of foreign missions is to make the Lord Jesus Christ known to all men as their Divine Saviour and to persuade them to become his disciples; to gather these disciples into Christian churches which shall be self-propagating, self-supporting, and self-governing; to cooperate as long as necessary with these churches in the evangelizing of their countrymen and in bringing to bear on all human life the spirit and principles of Christ."

Thus the purpose of missions, after having persuaded men and women to accept Christ as their personal Saviour, is to gather and organize them into Christian churches. The gospel is a message of redemption to men, but our responsibility does not stop when they are converted and baptized. Our ultimate aim is to build up the church of Christ in every land. The duty of the shepherd is not only to bring the lost sheep into the fold, but to care for the flock and provide for their spiritual nourishment.

Some people have a misconception of what the church is; for them a Christian is only a person who goes to church, hears sermons, and receives sacraments. No wonder some think that one can be a Christian without joining a church. Dr. A. G. Hebert says about the church, "It is a body with one life flowing through all the members; it is a temple, built up of living stones . . . it is the bride of Christ, united to him in love; it is the flock of the Great Shepherd; it is the family which together says 'Our Father.' " [1]

For Roman Catholics the church exists wherever the priest is present to administer the sacraments. The Roman priest introduces with himself in his office the church and its authority. He comes in Africa to persuade Africans to join the church that exists independently of them. But where the church is the body of believers, those believers are responsible for its governance as Christians. A missionary may have worked many years in a certain area, but he can claim a church only when he has been able to gather a group of believers possessing some capability of administering the spiritual welfare of their group. The very idea of church implies a sense of responsibility on the part of its members.

How significant in this respect is the rebuff from the Pope on the occasion of the World Congress of the Apostolate of the Laity on October 14, 1951. Rejecting a plea for the emancipation of the laity he said bluntly that this tendency was "hardly pleasing to us; it has rather an unpleasant sound." [2] If in all things the believers are subordinated to the ecclesiastical hierarchy, is it likely that the church will be an instrument of greatest progress in Africa? Just a glance at Africa shows the difference of development between backward Portuguese colonies where Roman Catholicism, teaching subjection to the clergy, is in power and the forward moving British territories, for example, where Protestant missions, foster-

[1] "The Mission of the Church," in *International Review of Missions*, p. 391, October, 1951.

[2] New York *Times*, October 15, 1951.

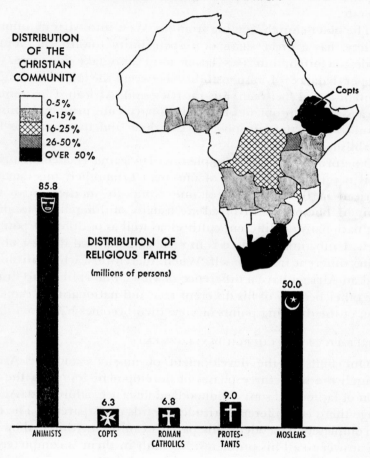

RELATIVE FAITHS IN AFRICA

DISTRIBUTION OF THE CHRISTIAN COMMUNITY

- 0-5%
- 6-15%
- 16-25%
- 26-50%
- OVER 50%

Copts

DISTRIBUTION OF RELIGIOUS FAITHS

(millions of persons)

85.8	6.3	6.8	9.0	50.0
ANIMISTS	COPTS	ROMAN CATHOLICS	PROTES-TANTS	MOSLEMS

GRAPHICS INSTITUTE, N.Y.C.

ing the sense of individual responsibility of believers, are free to operate.

The older church, coming from the West into African animistic society, has a great share of responsibility toward the younger African church, but this latter must also take its share. The proper balance of responsibility between the older and newer churches, and between missionaries and African Christians, is always a basic problem of the missionary enterprise and must remain so until the mission's work is done and the church is fully established.

The problem is not a simple one. Diverting elements enter in. It is not just the relation of one man to another, missionary to African in this case, nor of one group to another, mission to church. The parties involved are usually of different races, different nationalities, different cultures, as well as of different points of view. Unfortunately there is in man some natural distrust of anything different from himself. When, therefore, a white missionary and an African have a difference of views, one is likely to distrust the other because of his different race and nationality. Reconciliation of the differing points of view then becomes harder.

THREE PHASES OF CHURCH DEVELOPMENT

One finds in the development of missions and the African church the same three phases of development found in the relation of father and son: childhood, adolescence, adulthood. At each stage there is a different attitude towards one's parents. The child is completely dependent; his parents can do anything; they have an answer to all his problems; his faith in them is complete. The adolescent begins to sense his own strength; he questions his parents and all society; he frequently finds fault with everything done by people before him. Very often it is a rebellious age. In adulthood the son outgrows his negative attitude: "the old man was not so bad after all"; he and his parents live in mutual understanding and appreciation. Financially, the child depends wholly on his parents; the adolescent, while still needing his parents' help, begins to earn part of the costs; and the adult stands on his own, supports himself and his family. There is some parallel to this as the African churches grow bit by bit in their relations with missions and missionaries.

In the childhood stage the African church looks to others for all its needs, for funds and for leadership. Many churches in Africa are still in this stage. In the second stage the church, while still dependent on the mission for leadership and counsel, begins to do more of the work and to supply part of its own funds. It becomes restive under the authority of the mission; it wants more say in the direction of its own affairs. In the third stage the church attains full maturity in matters of administration and finances. It becomes self-propagating, self-supporting, self-governing. It may still, for a while, lack high standards and an understanding of its place in the world Christian movement. That can come only by further experience and growth.

The adolescent stage is often the hard one. Its length depends both on the capability and devotion of African Christians, and on the willingness and wisdom of foreign Christians in sharing and finally in surrendering responsibilities to the maturing group of African believers.

Some missionaries still seem to work on the assumption that Africans are children, or that they are backward, and that it will be a long time before they can take any major responsibility in the church. It is quite clear that Africans are in some ways different from Westerners. But it is also clear that there are great differences among Africans, as among Westerners. There is no dead-level of accomplishment among them even now, and modern education and opportunities are revealing the usual proofs of man's ability for high performance. To think or to act as though Africans are unable to understand and undertake the work of the Christian church today would be to deny the power of the Holy Spirit and to forget the lesson of growth and development of the early church, and of the church in every land. Fortunately many missionaries do not forget nor deny the power of the spirit and the lessons of history. And they feel their own knowledge of Africans reveals great potentials.

Some churches in Africa are in the adult stage, fully responsible for their own government and financial support. This desirable achievement, however, does not automatically mean in Africans' minds that missionaries are no longer necessary, desired, nor helpful. This in itself reveals something of the wisdom and capacity of the African and his judgment. For the African church in the third stage will continue to need the right missionaries as friends and counselors, as aides in the training for the ministry, and in Christian higher schools of several kinds. It is even barely possible, under some rulers, that Africans may wish Protestant missionaries with the right qualities to stand with them for a time in relations with government and other bodies.

This problem of building up an indigenous African church and helping to solve its difficulties of human relationships is the most important task Christian missions face in Africa. The solution of the problem lies in the partnership of missionaries who understand all the implications of their calling and of Africans who are committed pioneers in a new Christian way of life with their people.

The concept of true Christian community in Africa, with its inclusiveness comparable to that of the Palestinian gospel and to helpful African communal experience today, means that the ups and downs of Africans in their new economic and political relationships will be intimately related in their thinking to their own new spiritual developments. It is not natural for Africans to divide secular concerns from spiritual. In fact, the whole concept of "secular" as we often use it in the West is foreign to African thinking. I doubt that in any African language there is to be found a word expressing that peculiar Western concept of "secular." For in traditional African life the spirit seeks to comprehend, permeate, and guide all.

Thus it is that the new political and economic developments in the Gold Coast, for example, are likely to have further direct effect on the strengthening of the African church there. Or put it the other way round: the growth and responsibility of the African church in the Gold Coast is having direct effect on the strengthening of the economic and political life of the people. Or perhaps a possible African way of expressing it would be the best of all: the life of our people—spiritual, economic, political—is growing stronger and better in our new day. However expressed, the fact of interaction is there.

SELF-RULE

Because of this fact of interaction one ventures to introduce here, into a chapter on the church, some words on politics and economics. In Africa, in their innermost reactions, they are not easily separable. Perhaps in some other parts of the world they have become too easily separable.

The most progressive territory in Africa south of the Sahara probably is the Gold Coast. We may be having a preview there of what will happen, in some form or other, in every other territory in Africa.

For about fifty years marked progress has been made in the Gold Coast. There is perhaps no other part of Africa that in this period has been more fortunate in its people, its government, its resources, its church—and in the combination of all of them. Then early in 1948 disorders occurred; six members of the United Gold Coast Convention were arrested, including its leader, Mr. Kwame Nkrumah. These riots and deaths gave a profound shock to many foreigners and probably to some Africans. The Gold Coast had seemed better off, advancing faster and more smoothly in relations between the governing and the governed than any other part of colonial Africa. Then this blow-up! What did it mean?

A Royal Commission of Enquiry was dispatched to investigate the complex causes of these disturbances. The commission reported that the root of the dissatisfaction was "the suspicion which surrounds Government activity of any sort." [1] To overcome this distrust the report suggested an attack on the three main causes: political, economic, and social.

The commission's recommendation concerning reform of the Constitution was later studied by a local committee composed of thirty-eight members, all Africans, under the chairmanship of an African judge, Mr. Justice J. H. Coussey. Most of the recommendations of the Coussey report were later accepted by the British government. A new Constitution was proclaimed by the Governor on January 1, 1951. Its main features are a single Legislative Assembly and an Executive Council.

The Legislative Assembly is composed of eighty-four members. Seventy-five are Africans and elected by the people. The other nine members are either ex-officio or elected by the Chambers of Commerce and of Mines; of them, only two can vote.

---

[1] *Colonial Office Report of the Commission of Enquiry into Disturbances in the Gold Coast*, 1948, No. 231.

Of the eleven members of the Executive Council eight are Africans elected from the Assembly. These eight African members have ministerial status. They are in charge of the following departments: Development; Health and Labor; Education and Social Welfare; Agriculture and Natural Resources; Commerce, Industry, and Mines; and Local Government. Two are without portfolio.

The country-wide election held from February 5 to 10, 1951, was the first such among Africans in any part of the continent. It was a victory for Mr. Nkrumah's party. As soon as the results were known, the Governor released Kwame Nkrumah, whose jail term was not due to end until November, 1951.

At the same time Mr. James Griffiths, secretary of state for the colonies, sent from Britain the following message: "It is no light burden that the people of the Gold Coast are undertaking. The Governor and his officers are there to advise and guide them. . . . But it lies with the Africans themselves to prove their capacity for self-government and it is by their performance above everything else that the future course of advancement . . . will be determined, not only in the Gold Coast but elsewhere. . . ."

On February 26 the Legislative Assembly met and by secret ballot elected the eight African ministers. Mr. Nkrumah was elected unanimously except for one vote. Within the Executive Council in order of precedence first comes the Chief Secretary (the Minister for Defense and External Affairs, one of the three British ex-officio members); second, the Leader of Government Business (Mr. Nkrumah).[1]

Thus within a few years the Gold Coast has advanced up the road from colonialism far toward self-government. The Governor

[1] *Self-Rule in Africa*, by John R. E. Carr-Gregg, No. 473, New York, Carnegie Endowment for International Peace, 1951.

[101]

still has Britain's reserve powers enabling him to give effect of law to a bill rejected by the Assembly or to refuse approval of a law passed by it. A next step toward self-government would be to obtain dominion status. When Mr. Nkrumah was released from jail he made the following statement: "I come out of gaol and into the Assembly without the slightest feeling of bitterness to Britain," adding that the Gold Coast would remain within the British Commonwealth. On March 5, 1952, with the approval of Queen Elizabeth II, Mr. Nkrumah was named Prime Minister. He is the first African in history to become Prime Minister in the Western political pattern.

It is an error of large dimensions to think of the church in the Gold Coast as unrelated to this political and economic development. The Gold Coast church has progressed rather farther in its own full Christian responsibilities than has much of the African church elsewhere. The Ewe Church is an example. For many years it has been fully independent, continuing in effective collateral relations with foreign missionary bodies. The Gold Coast Christian Council has recently elected an African to its paid top secretaryship—the first time in Africa. The state of the church in the Gold Coast could not fail to be one of the strong interacting influences on political and economic developments. It is natural for Africans to think of everything as related to the spiritual.

The degree of realization or nonrealization of Africans' political and economic goals elsewhere in Africa will surely be felt in church matters also. In Nigeria an elaborate federal scheme of progress toward self-government by its 22 million people is being put into effect. A few more than half of the people are Moslem; to them Islam and politics and economics are already all closely tied. Likewise Christians and animists will consider their political and economic advance related to spiritual concerns.

Libya is already "free." Italian Somaliland will be in nine years. Tunisia wishes to be right now. And Morocco likewise. The Sudan is reaching for independence. Africans in the Union of South Africa are, on the contrary, well-nigh in despair. For all of them, these political and economic and social problems are deeply spiritual as well. Wherever the Christian church exists in Africa it is, whether Westerners like it or not, right in the middle of the peoples' lives, their loves, their hopes, their fears, their earnings, their hunger, their politics, their disease, their all. For to them life is whole. Religion is in it. The Christian church cannot yet pull itself out by any appeal to a Western separatism between the "spiritual" and the "secular." Such separation seems specious, indeed quite wrong to Africans.

This does not mean, as I understand traditional African views of life, that the church must become earthy or sullied or debased. Nor must it become subordinated to other elements of life. Far from it. It means that the spiritual must take its rightful place in life; it is the illuminator, the guide, the controlling power in all life.

The urge for self-government, coupled with a spiritual expectancy like this, becomes a tremendous challenge to the church. A growing African consciousness is found everywhere in Africa at different stages in church affairs as well as in politics. A slogan of the Gold Coast election campaign was, "We prefer self-government in danger to servitude with tranquility." Others put it: "We want freedom, even to make our own mistakes." "It is not in the nature of man to put up with subjection for too long." Similar basic feelings are undoubtedly in the minds of African Christians in regard to the church, which almost everywhere seems to them to be still pretty largely a white-controlled power. It is the responsibility of the church to give to the new leaders in this new life—

[103]

church life and all other aspects of life—the Christian ideals, the Christian responsibility, so that the laws will be inspired by the spirit of Christian justice, that honesty and peace and progress will be the aims of government, church, society—the whole of life. Africa is on the march, for good or for bad. We should work hard and fervently pray that from within the church will come out the leaders of this land for the whole of life.

Knowing this "wholeness" of outlook of the African, there should be no surprise that the same strong desire for emancipation from foreign "outside" domination by missions and missionaries is found in the churches, as it is found in politics and economics. Have missions made plans to give satisfaction to the Africans for self-government in their churches and are they training the necessary responsible leadership?

In attempting to write on this critical question, as well as on others in this book, I am spiritually indebted to many friends, Africans and others, who have generously responded to my request for their views. It is significant that they are in general accord, and it is clear that there are some hopeful developments in some places.

But one must conclude that today the Protestant staff in Africa, overwhelmingly white at the top, is critically behind its duty in this matter of giving real responsibility to African Christians in the African church. These pages would scarce hold all the developed reasons, some of them persuasive reasons, for going slow, for being careful, for proceeding cautiously, thus preserving the purity of the church, preventing error, keeping the finances straight, and letting the Africans gain experience.

I make but one comment on this latter. The surest way to keep man from gaining experience is to prevent him from experiencing.

In all this hesitancy about Africans taking real responsibility in

[104]

the work of the Christian church is there not evidence of a serious lack of faith? Jesus got twelve men with him. About three years later eleven of them had, humanly speaking, to carry everything. Twenty centuries later we thank them and him for all the best we have in our lives. Jesus is still with us in North America and Europe. He is with us all in Africa, too. Our count—his may be different—shows he has about 21 million with him in Africa, beginning a hundred years or so ago. Surely the African church ought to be well on its own now, with its disciples going also into all the world.

Certainly there are difficulties. Education is one of them. There are not enough educated Christians. (One wonders a bit about the formal education of the twelve. It is certain, at least, that there wasn't a B.D. or a Ph.D. among them.) In any case, education is only preparation for the assumption of responsibility. Have educated African Christians been pressingly invited into true church responsibility? And given it? And allowed and encouraged to grow in it? Leaders grow by accepting and meeting responsibilities. There is no other way.

Financial insecurity is a difficulty also. A capable and well trained person who might accept a responsible position of leadership in the church may shrink before the small salary the free-will offerings of the church would give him. He could receive much more from government or business, paid out of taxes or trade profit.

But all the young ministry of the West is initially recruited despite that same difficulty. Is the young African Christian different? I doubt that he is. What is different is the church job offered him. With us the minister, the pastor, the priest is recognized by most Christians as holding the highest calling, sharing the great responsibilities of the community and the nation, occupying a position from which he can lead in almost anything—if he has the qualities. In the African church the invitation too often is to become the sub-assistant to a white foreigner. If you have to be a sub-assistant to a white foreigner anyway, why not do it in government or trade where at least the pay is good?

It seems to me as sure as anything is in human nature that the young educated African would respond about as the young educated North American does to a real challenge to Christian leadership among his people.

He might today respond even better. For he is in a continent where government and trade and science are all still predominantly white-foreigner controlled. He is in a society in which the spiritual penetrates and guides the whole of life. He wants a wholeness of life for himself and his children and his children's children. Where could he use his talent better to help build and assure that wholeness in the new life than right in the Christian ministry, in the freedom of the gospel, in the challenge which that freedom gives for spiritual revolution in the hearts of his people?

That is the challenge which, in Africa's present circumstances and no matter for what salary, might appeal to the young educated African enormously. But that is the challenge he doesn't get often enough in Africa today.

These and the other difficulties involved are before us as Christians for solution. Some churches are finding the solution. But one seems to see many more whose minds say, "Wait. Go slow."

Those same words were long heard on foreigners' lips in Japanese and in all the Chinese dialects, and the Indian and the Malayan. Those are right words at right times. But they are rapidly losing their rightness in these times in Africa.

Africans feel they are beginning to move Africa. Christianity has been the greatest power in stirring them and educating them and getting them on the move. They feel that growing power within them. Many of them see clearly that the Christian church can be the powerhouse of God on earth. But if they come to feel that in the church they are doomed to be but subassistants to the white foreigners forever—and in the fast-moving days of African youth even a short time that is too long can seem forever —the church will undoubtedly lose place, people, and power in these formative days of African new life.

The foreign contribution to the solution of this problem in Africa is the missionary. "What type of new missionaries does this awakening Africa need?" was recently asked of an experienced Africa missionary.[1] His answer was: "The best." A few years ago the feeling in some circles was: "Anyone who is willing to go is good enough. Africa is such a backward continent, anyway!" This is not and never has been true. But the unfortunate thing is that a good number of missionaries have gone out with that idea apparently in mind. They have felt they heard the call. With little inquiry into further qualifications or preparation they have gone.

The development of African church leadership depends at this stage in great measure on the type and quality of the missionaries at work. The whole matter of proper missionary qualifications and preparation cannot be dealt with in this book. But we might examine it briefly in respect to the problem of development of African leadership in the church.

All-important are the right motives. The first and basic motive is obedience to the command of God to proclaim the message of salvation and to organize the believers into churches. The second, love, is the creative motive. This love is not pity, for pity carries often an idea of superiority and condescension toward the less

[1] Ray E. Phillips.

[107]

fortunate. This creative love is certainly not philanthropy. This constraining love is "disinterested love, spontaneous, creative, free, vicarious, sacrificial!" [1] We have it for the African if the love of God has really laid hold of us. The African will more readily understand that love of God through demonstration in our lives than through verbal and doctrinal explanation of it.

Missionaries must have good professional preparation. The day of the Jack-of-all-trades is over. But the prepared specialist must also be prepared to serve if needed at anything within his power— even though he may think at first he hasn't the power. For above everything the missionary must be prepared to *serve*.

Coupled with right motives and proper preparation are right attitudes toward the men and women of Africa.

The missionary who best helps the development of a strong free church in Africa is he who unmistakably has first in his heart loyalty to his calling and to his African brethren. We have heard an African say of a missionary: "This man is an American first and a Christian second." The missionary was so very proud of the superiority of the American way of life. The question rose in others' minds as to where his real loyalty lay. A man may have pride of country. But a missionary's first loyalty is to his Lord and the people whom he serves. If that is not clear, all else can be clouded. Missionaries cannot afford a provincial mind. They must be able to cross all boundaries, racial, national, denominational —all.

MISSIONARY MOTIVATION

The love and loyalty motivating missionary service requires identification with the people loved. God has shown his love to

---

[1] "The Missionary Vocation," by Tracey K. Jones, Jr., in *International Review of Missions*, p. 404, October, 1951.

us by identifying himself with our human nature. In the same manner the only effective missionary is the one who is willing to identify himself with the Africans, their joys, their sorrows and tribulations, and perhaps especially with their aspirations. He must be willing to see things not from the North American nor the European point of view, but from the African point of view. Some missionaries have interpreted this identification with the Africans to mean that they had to "go native." Such interpretation is one that probably no African either understands or appreciates. Neither does it mean that the missionaries will agree with all African opinions or back them in all their claims. The Africans are as prone to err as are other men and women. The missionaries can be critical, but they must always seek to have understanding and to be sympathetic. Other expressions of love are the desire to put the others' interest higher than one's own and the joy in seeing the others grow, even at the cost of self-denial. The true missionary can sincerely use the words of John the Baptist to say of the African church: It must increase, but I must decrease.

The deep sense of oneness within the African church must be nurtured. There was a missionary whose home church held as essential the practice of baptism by immersion. He went to West Africa with colleagues for new work among the people of a small tribe hitherto untouched by the gospel. Their field was surrounded by larger tribes, among whom were working other missionaries who administered baptism by sprinkling. When time came for the baptism of the first converts after the arrival of the new missionary, he felt that by insisting on a form of baptism different from that generally followed in the area he would disturb the mind of the Africans. He and his colleagues consulted on this problem. They were not unanimous, but decided to defer decision and pray for guidance until they could be of one mind. Several

[109]

months of prayer followed. They were led to decide, unanimously, to baptize by sprinkling. Here was a case in which a missionary was led to surrender a cherished practice for a higher loyalty—the oneness of Christ's church in Africa.

Western Protestant denominationalism seems largely to have grown in response to particular stimuli in a particular society in a particular time in history. Its body of agreements in the gospel remains much larger than the sum of its particularisms. The realization of this is enormously important. That realization seems somewhat clearer and easier, fortunately, when the denominations meet in another and non-Christian society, in another and most critical time, and experience other and very powerful spiritual stimuli—all of those stimuli strengthening, clearly, their body of agreements in Christ for the salvation of the world.

Therein lies the reason why greater Christian functional cooperation and unity have always, in the era of modern missions, first occurred in "foreign" fields rather than at "home."

The ills of ignorance, superstition, and unbelief in non-Christian lands can be remedied only from within. Christian knowledge, love, faith, and belief can cure those ills and reach the soul within only if the fullest power of Christ is present. Lesser denominational efforts may strive bravely against those ills. But the remedy that can certainly cure them is the living power pouring freely from the whole body of Christ—his church on earth.

In considering Africa we need to remember that our Christianity in the West has come to us largely through Graeco-Roman channels, and that we see it with our Western eyes. Western culture is by no means synonymous with Christianity. There is much in African culture that is precious to Africans and is not opposed to Christianity. Our task in Africa is to try to make Christ and his saving love known to Africans, and to help African believers, accepting Christ in their hearts, to build their church of Christ. To begin with, they may accept certain Western denominational forms even though they do not fully understand them—as many do not really understand, either, the Protestant-Catholic divisions. But in the end it must be expected that there will grow an African church.

A wise father does not ask a copy of himself from his son. A great teacher requests no replica from his student. The wisest Father of us all and the greatest Teacher who ever lived asked man to be true to himself, his God, and his fellow men. That is the African's Christian charter. It is ours as well, and Japan's, and China's, and every man's.

When all the temptations of secularism, of nationalism, of communism, and the constant pull of animism assail the young churches, the missionary by his understanding, his vision, and his selflessness must be a proof that Christianity is not bound by the barriers of denominationalism, race, nationality, or culture. He must testify by deeds to the universality of the church. His authority comes from no denomination, from no function, and from no rank nor class nor calling. It comes only from his faithfulness as a true servant and witness of that Christ whose love embraces all, whose power enables all, and whose spirit can render useful an infinite variety of man's works.

The gospel is a revolutionary book. If Christians take its message for what it is, they must be revolutionary minded. The very purpose of the Christian mission is change. The whole mind and reflex of the missionary must be geared to change, not only to spiritual change but to change in every realm of life. Labor, industry, trade, science, welfare, mass education, marriage, the home, the land, the cities, water power, mining, transportation, literature, medicine, recreation, politics, race, religion—everything in

[111]

Africa is in change. The Western Christian mission has been a tremendous force in getting this change going. The African Christian church has a greater role: to illumine, shape, guide, and use this change for God's glory, the saving oneness with him of his people.

The Book-of-the-Month Club chose last winter Supreme Court Justice William O. Douglas' *Strange Lands and Friendly People*.[1] Among other things he says that what Americans can do to save Asia is to "emulate the teachers and the missionaries, identify ourselves with the aspirations of the peasants, and help them by kindness and understanding to achieve a fuller life." Justice Douglas sees clearly that in the heart of the Christian mission and Christian action lies the hope of the underdeveloped peoples of the world.

The hope indeed lies there. And the completest fulfillment of that hope lies in the establishment, growth, and ascending service of the Christian church in every land, by every people, to serve man's every need everywhere.

A strong, free church is Africa's basic need. All missionaries recognize this. That is their purpose in Africa. They give their lives for it. Their home churches support them in it. I am one of them. But there are always dangers in life. I mention but three. One is conformity. One is conservancy. One is complacency. They all have good points. Singly they have some usefulness. But triply linked they can be terrible.

Triply they have been linked, in church and out, in a good many countries, especially in countries and among people that were having things pretty good. Canada and the United States are two of those countries. The United Church of Canada has been looking into this and other matters. In 1950, it published *The*

[1] New York, Harper and Brothers, 1951.

For a Strong, Free Church

Church and the Secular World. That title might not be so well understood in cultures where religion is not so sharply divided from the rest of life. But much of what the book said could be very well understood anywhere. It said that Christianity had been an inspiration in all Western social progress. But it said communism was the proof that the church had lagged and that the people had begun to look elsewhere for the cure of their social ills. The church, instead of reaching out, had curled up in self-satisfaction. It had fallen into the temptation "to organize itself as a secure society of the saved, rather than an adventurous society of the saving, and to screen its members in terms of their spiritual accomplishments rather than in terms of their spiritual needs." [1]

That is a valuable word for all of us regarding Africa. The challenging need of African Christians and of Africa is a strong church, and a free church. To be truly strong and free in Africa, it must be African. And it must be an adventurous society of the saving, concerned with the saving of the whole of life.

For above all the African senses that it is the spirit alone that can embrace and direct the whole of life, and that only in this wholeness can man gain his fullest heights.

[1] *The Church and the Secular World*. The United Church of Canada, 1950.

Chapter Six

NORTH AMERICA'S RESPONSIBILITY

IT SEEMS TO ME IMPOSSIBLE HERE TO ASSESS QUANTITATIVELY THE load North America is to bear as its part in the Western coopera- tion and the Christian building in Africa today.

But qualitatively I should like to try. For the quality, the type of load North America can well bear in aid of Africa, seems to me clear and greatly needed.

The support for this load is of three kinds, a tripod. On uneven ground a tripod is the most easily adjusted and the most stable bearer of loads. And everyone knows there is uneven ground in Africa. But when three legs support a load, every leg must be good. If one leg goes the load goes, too. In Africa all three legs must be good or the load is not borne.

The three legs of this North American load are: (1) political and economic measures; (2) technology and know-how; (3) Chris- tian gospel and community.

Only brief mention of political and economic measures is pos- sible. But this part of the load has very special historical and emotional elements in it for North America.

For one thing, both Canada and the United States have been

[114]

colonies. They have come out of the colonial status by two different doors, the commonwealth door and the independence door. These doors, it turns out, have brought them into the same room —the room where Canada is in the commonwealth with Britain but independent, and where America is independent but in the commonweal with Britain. This experience of two neighbors has its significance for neighbors in Africa and the presently ruling powers: that no nation wins complete freedom in today's world, and that all freedom-loving peoples must have one another.

A second thing is that the United States and Canada have no territorial stakes in Africa and very little financial stake. Neither have they long held other peoples in colonial status against their wills. They have both had the experience of being colonial powers and of freely giving freedom.

Another thing: North America has with Africa a 16-million-person tie, unique among nations. Despite its inhuman and sinful beginnings, this tie is now precious and its problems are in solution. Such problems can be solved, here and everywhere.

And lastly in this political context, Canada and the United States give an example unique in history of free nations with 3,000 miles of common boundary across which, since the earliest days, no shot has been fired in anger and where only tiny formalities are necessary in crossing. All four of these North American experiences have political significance for Africa.

On the economic side, some United States and Canadian aid will be needed in Africa to supplement European funds. Such aid will probably be fully reimbursed in the future if Africa is drawn into the peace-loving company of nations where Africa would naturally want to be.

In the United Nations and in every international relation Canada and the United States have a special reason, right, and duty to stand politically and economically for Africa's best interests, remembering their own past and the blessings that are now theirs. Abstentions in critical ballots and negative votes when Africans' rights are clearly at stake are acts that our two countries should repent and do no more forever. We shall not in the end gain Western solidarity by African disillusionment. Instead, political influence and economic aid for Africa's best interests should be a fixed policy for both our lands. In this we should steadily support all sound liberal groups and moves in the European governing nations. They see vividly, as we should, the sort of three-dimensional "methods" picture in Asia today: France and Indo-China; the Netherlands and the East Indies; Britain and India-Ceylon. Here are perspectives for all to study. We should work with Europeans and Africans for steady progress in African development and toward self-government. Our heritage alone should lead us thus. But if heritage cannot do it, then self-interest should. For Africa will be a powerful ally of someone in the future.

The second of the three legs supporting the load is technology and know-how. To emphasize this element of solid support for the total load must be nearly needless. For here is the most backward of large lands, with volumes yet needing to be done, and with people eager for the doing and for the profit from it.

Two things in this matter of technology and know-how we should first recognize and appreciate at their true value, one good and one otherwise.

The first is that certain governments are pressing forward with technological instruction and performance, and have been working at it for a good many years in Africa. North Americans should never think that the whole of Africa is virgin territory for technical skills and production. In some areas a good deal has been done, and against great odds. The financial burden of the doing

[116]

has been heavy. It is possible that if human emotions and international ideologies did not enter in, something like the pace already set in these development plans in some areas would now suffice, and the eventual technical results might possibly be even better and more generally assimilated and shared by the people, with less dislocation and resulting confusion, than by a great speed-up.

But, understandably, human emotions and international ideologies have entered in. The situation is no longer under the same local control as in the past. The whole world tempo is stepped up. Parts of Africa have been swept into that tempo. It may surprise Africans and catch them unprepared. But they grow to like the tempo, for they feel the beat quicken and the steps accelerate toward the goal of freedom and self-government. In advance of experiencing it they may misjudge what freedom means and what self-government demands. But never mind, they think, others have it and seem to survive somehow. Let us have it, too!

Under these circumstances no colonial power—Britain, for example—weakened domestically and globally by two world wars, can find all the money and all the technical personnel required for all the speeded-up development of all its territories in Africa. Neither is it prepared, for various reasons, to relinquish those territories either to another power (even if there were a suitable and willing one to take over) or to an international authority like the UN (even if the latter were receptive). The alternative is either to keep the present slower rate of progress or to invite in outside capital and know-how to supplement its efforts.

There are other powers in Africa, however, who have made it quite clear that while they may or may not be willing to accept American money and matériel, they have no need, or at least no desire, for American know-how contributed in the persons of Americans.

There are still others who want neither American government money nor Americans.

In this whole realm of technology and know-how, and especially in the basic preparation of people for it, North American Christians, as private citizens, face one of the truly great challenges of history, and as Christians they face it down three avenues: the avenue of industry, the avenue of philanthropy, the avenue of missions.

THE AVENUE OF INDUSTRY

Certain units in North American industry have, at home, gone further in general aid of man and community at large than industry has anywhere else. These industries think, in general, that this has "paid." The why and how of its paying is exceedingly complex. Indeed so is man, and society. All life is complex.

But there are two elements in this complex that are always present if such aid pays its highest. One is sincerity. The industry must have, and must convince the community that it has, sincerity in any welfare and public service work it undertakes. And sincerity in such work usually includes a degree of self-interest, for self-interest in its unassailable form is that interest which is also the best interest of one's fellows. Such self-interest, candidly coupled with other honest objectives, helps greatly to create group acceptance of the sincerity of the industry involved.

The other element, which sincerity helps create, is confidence. When sincerity produces, confidence is a product. Such sincerity and confidence together can enable a business in North America to render service to man and community far beyond the material product of its output. But the material product usually increases also, for any true good in human society helps almost everyone.

Now this plus service by North American and by all other

[118]

Western industry in Africa, in addition to giving decent wages and working conditions, is the one sure means by which industry, and capitalism its father, can win not only the man-hours and physical skills but also the spiritual assent and loyalty of Africans throughout Africa. For Africans are impressed by the technology and know-how of the West and by what it produces materially. They want these.

But long and unhappy experiences with Western industry leave them little belief in its sincerity in any plus service for man and community in Africa, even where some such services may exist. And without belief in industry's sincerity, confidence cannot grow. And where confidence—and resultant loyalty—is not, communism can come.

If North American industry, now slowly interesting itself in Africa and using there its best designs for material production, would tool up and work there also from its best designs for personal and community service, it would convincingly serve its own best interests, the best interests of the African people, and the very best interests of the whole world on the side of the Christian-founded democratic West.

Nowhere is there a large area and a great population more needy for and at the same time more open to an approach of this kind from Western industry. And in such an approach North America bears large responsibility. For substantial sections of its industry possess a three-way experience not excelled anywhere: an advanced technology; the basic principles of an excellent know-how that can be adapted to African conditions and utilized by Africans; and a plus service to man and community that, wisely applied in African society, could have constructive effects in this uncertain world beyond our present imagining.

[119]

THE AVENUE OF PHILANTHROPY

Some months ago a Frenchman on his home soil said to me, "Look, we really can't understand America. We can't even understand the Marshall Plan gifts to France, much as we like them. Why does America give all these goods and dollars away? What's the hidden hook we swallow with this bait? We can't see it, but it *must* be there!"

And another, in the same vein, added, "Perhaps we can't quite understand all this because we don't really understand your private philanthropy in America. Giving all those millions away every year—Rockefeller, Carnegie, Guggenheim, Mellon, Whitney, Field, Rosenwald, Sage, Harkness, Phelps-Stokes, all those new ones in Texas—and now Ford!"

We needn't expect that the avenue of philanthropy in Africa will be without its chuckholes and bumps. Nevertheless North America, because of the very existence of philanthropy on the scale it has here, and because of Africa's present state, should use this avenue of philanthropy in bearing North America's share of the load in Africa.

There are already footpaths of American philanthropy in Africa along which avenues may grow. These footpaths are important, and lead into the very beings of many Africans. They are the efforts that have been made to banish malaria and sleeping sickness and leprosy and yellow fever from their bodies; to battle illiteracy in their society; to buttress education; to build understandings and undertakings through selective exchanges of persons— Africans, Europeans, and North Americans—to consult, observe, and study in one another's countries.

But these, by any measurement, are only footpaths now. The avenues are yet to be built. One large foundation has a special section concerned with a part of Africa—the British dominion and colony part. Another has provided a number of scholarships through the years for music, art, and literature. A third has done its most in medicine. A smaller one has contributed very significantly to educational methods. But not one has made Africa its general concern—or if one has, recently, it is not yet into its avenue-building stride.

Africa is right now in a critically recipient state of mind regarding North American philanthropic aid. It is in two states, as a matter of fact—the state of mind of governments, and the state of mind of Africans. Those two states of mind by no means always coincide.

Governments are split among themselves on the matter. Probably the British are more receptive to the idea of rightly directed American philanthropic aid than any of the other colonial powers. But even local British colonial governments are not a unit on this, I should judge. And each British colonial unit has much autonomy.

Africans generally, who know something of the outside world, seem to have few doubts about the desirability of North American philanthropy. There must be several thousand letters a year to North America from Africans seeking such philanthropy—for books, Bibles, fountain pens, bicycles, and education—especially education. There are more than eight hundred African students now in North America, every one of them, I should judge, receiving some degree of philanthropic aid from individuals, communities, schools, churches, or other organizations.

Generally speaking, the avenue of philanthropy appears open to North America in Africa. But it needs additional informed, wise, and hard-headed builders in its making. It is easier for philanthropy than for our governments to deal with the often conflicting factors of government and people in Africa. But it is by no means simple; wisdom backed by determination is needed—as for any road building anywhere. If intelligently followed and wisely coordinated, this avenue of philanthropy can be a great contribution to African advancement, to world understanding, and to peaceful cooperation and production.

For a variety of reasons, this is a broad and beckoning avenue, this avenue of philanthropy for aiding the advance of a whole people, just emerging from animistic communalism, toward the dangerous but challenging goals of modern technology and know-how. It will not soon be crowded, this avenue. But nevertheless it must be an avenue with real depth and breadth, for its future is forever. The spirit of philanthropy, of selfless helping of one another—that is one of the indispensables of life. That is one of the great challenges for Africa—that Africans themselves in the days ahead will travel this avenue for others.

THE AVENUE OF THE CHRISTIAN MISSION

The avenues of industry and of philanthropy are important, indeed indispensable in North America, in helping Africans receive and absorb the complexities of technology and know-how. But the third avenue is even more important. For it is the basic creator of the best in the other two. Without it industry and philanthropy have never, anywhere, developed the special qualities that give them greatest appeal and loyalty from the hearts of men. And without it man does not know what to do with technology and know-how when he gets it.

This third avenue is the avenue of the Christian mission in the world. This avenue comes straight up the third of the three legs required to carry the load that North America bears regarding Africa—the Christian gospel and community. Let us use the final words of this book to speak about the North American responsibility for the Christian gospel and community in Africa, and in the whole world where Africa and North America are. For it is straight from the Christian gospel and community that the avenue of the Christian mission comes.

Most readers of this book will know the essential principles of the Christian gospel. But let us define again, for this summing up, what is meant by Christian community as used so often herein. It is that group of Christians, whether in daily touch or seeing one another rarely or never, who each in his daily, his hourly life seeks humbly and earnestly to follow Christ's teaching and example in every act, to put Christ's teaching and example into practice in every thing he is called to do. No one ever succeeds fully. But it is the one who tries consciously, humbly, and ceaselessly who is in the Christian community in that special sense in which those two words are here used.

For him the "secular" is also "spiritual." The spiritual moves the whole of life. The spiritual is not a fuzzy, emotional pervasion. It is a clear, hard-headed reality. We may not always interpret it aright. But when we get its true leading, life finds for us its true direction and directives. The secular then gets new power. Science, technology, know-how, the atom, all become tools under right directives. The direction is toward the good of all. God is the father of this all, its Creator. And through Jesus Christ is its revelation and man's salvation. Such is the Christian community here spoken of. It is within the whole world. Within it is the whole of life.

We have spoken of the three legs that support the load North America bears in relation to Africa. In truth I see but one—the Christian gospel and community. For if it had no existence, no reality, if it possessed no allegiance and no obedience, North America, Africa, and the world would almost certainly today be

[123]

a jungle, a shambles, without challenging plan, without sustaining hope, without that enabling spirit that powers man and society to accomplish its miracles of change and advance in each generation. For in essence man is spirit. And the only spiritual philosophy and community that has its roots and group in every country of the world, the one that has won more allegiance among more peoples than any other and powered the greatest advances made by man—that is the Christian gospel and community.

It has been the great power for change in Africa in the past century. At today's stage in African and world affairs it is of the greatest importance that men and women of the West recognize and remember this, and likewise this further fact: that this power for change has applied itself in two ways, one direct, the other indirect.

The indirect application has been the strong and persistent power of the Christian ethic in forming and developing Western life, even though often temporarily checked; and the very considerable part played by this Christian ethic in the initial and then in the continuing Western contact with Africa. It was at the heart of the honest part of "the white man's burden" idea. That idea was poorly served from the very first by the gratuitous, unchristian insertion of the emphatic "white." Aiding others is man's burden. There have been tens of thousands of "whites" in Africa whose burdens have been greatly lightened by Africans; many whose lives Africans have saved; many, of whom I am one, whose spirits have been greatly broadened and lifted by Africans. Man's burden can be well borne only when borne by all. The Africans help bear man's burden, too.

This "burden" business in relation to Africa has brought discredit on itself by every element of selfishness (not self-interest, I suggest, as noted above), of discrimination, domination, and op-

[124]

pression that has wormed into it. But the core idea of serving others is an essential Christian principle. And the constant pressure and insistent corrective of the Christian conscience in the West and in the world has been the strongest moral force through the years in combatting the wrong and strengthening the good in foreigners' relationships with Africa.

A chief purpose of this present study of Africa by the churches of North America is to help enlighten and empower minds and hearts of Christians here in things that need to be done at home that are "indirectly" of direct influence on our whole world relationship to Africa. Among these things is greatly enlarged education of the North American public about Africa, its problems, aspirations, and potentials; bettered political backing of Africa's good in all of North America's relations with other countries; and very much more North American contribution to the economic and material development of Africa, with fullest African participation, responsibility, and benefit. It is in this way that the Christian ethic can have its continued and greatest indirect application for Africa's good, through the political and economic stimulus of the Western countries.

The direct application of the Christian gospel and community concept to Africa has been the theme of each page of this writing thus far. I shall not attempt recapitulation here. What more is to be done? What load now does North America bear? The six elements mentioned below are important for North America's own sake, and for Africa's. I hope they may be compelling for more Christians than ever before. I assure you they are not exhaustive; they are selective, from among many.

One. To know and understand and work with Africans in the building and extending of the Christian community in Africa is our basic requirement. Many North American Christians who cannot work in Africa can help meet that basic requirement by getting well acquainted with some of the eight hundred African students in a hundred or more communities right here at home. The impressions and effects of such friendships can be lasting for years ahead.

Two. Human rights are essential in Christian community. Racial prejudice, economic discrimination, political inequalities, church insensitivity, and social barriers are all enemies of human rights and of Christian community everywhere. Human rights form this year's home mission study theme. It is not coincidence that a home mission study affects the world. There is very little we do at home that does not affect the world. As never before in history, the world is a community. And human rights in a community are only as strong as the weakest right. In the Christian community they should be tops. In the world community they should be progressively lifted, every nation beginning at home.

Three. United functioning should greatly enlarge in a number of responsibilities within the Christian community. Some of these responsibilities are for preparation; some are for action. They all should contribute to a strong and constantly growing and rising African Christian church-and-community—while we should always remember, in our humiliation, that in our secularized West the Christian church and the Christian community (as defined in these writings) are seldom one. Let us consider briefly some of these responsibilities in which united functioning is further needed.

United training of the African ministry is perhaps the hardest of all functions of preparation in which to assure Western Christianity's effective cooperation. There is not yet much cooperation of that sort in training the African ministry. Many reasons can be and are put forward in explanation or excuse: (a) language and tribal differences; (b) low level of general education and pressing need of gospel presentation at once in hundreds of villages around each mission station, so that there are few prepared and to be "spared" for fuller Bible study and preparation in a cooperative central training school; (c) feeling, perhaps, that only the most rudimentary preparation is now required to minister to the primitive pagan people "in the bush"; (d) maybe in some cases a companion feeling that, after all, the chances of getting an African trained ministry in the near future are so remote and the chances of individual and group failures and aberrations are so great on the part of the African ministry that the best thing really is for the Western missionary to keep top responsibility in his own hands in the period just ahead, for the future safety and welfare of the Christian cause; (e) historic theological and denominational differences and the urge to assure the propagation of one's own church forms and doctrines; (f) nationalistic differences among Westerners; (g) clashes of personality and of practice; (h) staff shortages under tremendous current loads and resultant unwillingness to give up any top-hole personnel (Western or African) or money to a "united project"—a type of project that continues all too often in cooperative work to be regarded and referred to generally by boards and missions as something separate and different from "our own work"; (i) lack in some places of just the right person or persons, commanding wide confidence, to initiate and guide a project in the united training of the ministry.

These are all real problems. But a problem by very definition of the word is something proposed for solution. Various partial solutions, at least, have been found in some other continents. And certain tentative efforts in Africa give encouragement. But these are basic problems of the Christian church and community in Africa. They deserve a basic approach to a basic understanding and a basic solution. A beginning would be the clearance of what, from the spiritual viewpoint, are the lesser obstacles. Example: in one African area missions from two nations but of one denomination have found themselves, throughout their fifty-four years there together, unable to agree on united training of their own African ministry in the area. That cannot be due to a basic theological difference. Some observers believe it is due to personal and perhaps national differences, and to the fact that one mission permits tobacco smoking and the other does not.

The two highest-level recent approaches to united ministerial training in Africa have both come, in large degree, from outside the African church and mission. They are found in the two new university colleges in Nigeria and in the Gold Coast. Some of the local missions and churches are backing these two ventures, and some among them helped to initiate both. But it is a new "secular" agency, the university college in each instance, that seemed required to get things going.

Nowhere in non-British Africa has a comparable beginning been made for Protestant training. The Roman Catholics, however, have long since sufficiently overcome all their internal difficulties in this matter to be able to establish their usual and full seminary training procedures for African clergy for practically all their African areas. And we should not assume that they have no internal difficulties in this. For them the elements mentioned in (a), (b), (c), (d), (f) above are about as great as they are for Protestants. And as for (e), the differences and rivalries between the Roman Catholic orders and congregations are rather less known than among Protestants only because they have an authoritarian and hierocratical organization that generally curtains them. As for (g), clashes of personality, Roman Catholics are just as human as Protestants.

The Roman Catholics have probably been able and willing almost everywhere unitedly to give higher and earlier training and rank to their clergy than have Protestants because of one central factor: authority in the hierarchy channeled from the pope. This authority provides four necessary things: ability to capitalize and organize on the basis of long world-wide experience; ability to take all policy and action decisions at the top, if necessary; availability and flexibility of personnel and money from all over the world; unquestioned ultimate control at top and through an effective chain of command no matter how many African priests are formed and ordained, and made into bishops, or even archbishops and cardinals eventually. Protestants have none of these things to the same degree.

As an example of flexibility of personnel and money in an educational field other than that of the clergy, I recall how the Roman Catholics in the Belgian Congo years ago, in an industrial school they were running to train Africans with Lever Brothers' money on a large Lever palm oil plantation, required a priest or brother who was a skilled wrought-iron worker and a potter, and who spoke French and Flemish. Two or three months later he arrived, transferred from South America.

We Protestants have perhaps harder problems in this united training of the African ministry. The need is that much greater to solve them. North America has a special load in this in non-British African territory because we have rather larger forces there and the problem poses special facets that only coordinated national and international effort can tackle.

Four. A second united preparational need is as yet only partly met: specialized training of missionaries, both at home and in orientation centers in Europe.

There are three of the latter: Brussels (about 200 missionaries); Lisbon (about 40); Paris (about 130). The facilities are there; the staffs are competent; the results have proven themselves. The proficiency gained in the French and Portuguese languages, in the study of tropical medicine and hygiene and the methods of practice by our missionary doctors and nurses, and of educational methods and policies by our teachers have been fruitful. Some additional knowledge gained of colonial fiscal, land, and labor policies has been good additional preparation. Observance of Roman Catholic and Protestant relationships, and contact especially with evangelical groups in the three countries, should prove extremely valuable for the future.

The things that are further and especially needed are: (a) for additional boards to use these centers more systematically and for adequate periods of time; (b) for all boards and missions to urge upon their missionaries greater friendly contact with citizens of the three host countries; and (c) for more boards to contribute their suitable financial share to the maintenance of the centers.

This last item is an internal matter of not too great importance in the present three centers. But the principle is basic. Its acceptance has always to be voluntary in Protestant groups. Finances are unavoidably involved in all functional cooperation, and boards' constituencies are not to be kept in ignorance of that.

Five. A third united preparational need is of even broader scope. It is a need felt everywhere overseas, Africa included, where North Americans are to live and work in industry, banking, commerce, missions, government, education, research, Point IV, or in other tasks. It is the need to provide North American Christian men and women, training themselves in our countries for jobs in these lines, with not only top-hole professional and technical schooling and experience, but with a cultural and spiritual insight and understanding of ourselves and our society and of the people overseas with whom they will live and work.

In almost all the countries to which North American men and women go—in the Near, Middle, and Far East, Southeast Asia, Africa—there will be a spiritual core in the national life that will usually be more openly admitted and expressed than is our habit in Western society. It will in most cases not be Christian. But it will be spiritual. And it will be important and strong in many relations.

North Americans, no matter how excellent in their professions and technology, will use these abilities more creatively and transmit them more effectively if they have knowledge and understanding of how to relate their skills wherever possible in consonance rather than in conflict with the cultural and spiritual life of the people.

If such a relation in some cases proves impossible, they will be better equipped to try to find a new entrance into the life of their hosts if they know the latter's deep beliefs and if, as well, they are informed of the basis and the doings of their own cultural and religious heritage and are prepared to try to relate it in very practical ways to the needs of those about them.

For it should be remembered by every North American going abroad—or staying at home—that, of all the spiritual forces man has experienced, Christianity has fired more souls and helped more people than any religion among men. Christianity is not high-powered. But Christianity is very high power. And it is meant, and always ready, to be used to serve man and to be served by man.

Christianity is an asset for any person, for any nation. In today's struggle for the hearts and loyalties of men it has no equal. Without it the staggering productivity of our earth can destroy all its producers. With it, there can be brotherhood, regeneration, peace, and plenty. There are many people of the East and Africa, Christians and non-Christians, who know this, however dimly. They know our countries and people chiefly through our fellow citizens of many callings who live and work with them or in their midst. If through them they were convinced we knew it, too, a fateful page in history might be jointly turned and a new writing begun.

There are a dozen other major matters in which North America bears a load toward Africa. Medicine and public health; literacy and literature; great ranges in education; the wider and deeper preaching of the gospel in all the tongues to all the people—these tasks challenge our every strength.

The sixteen Christian councils in Africa are of strategic value in the united bearing of the load. The oldest regional Christian council in the world was formed in 1911 as the Congo Continuation Committee. At present, its successor, the Congo Protestant Council (which succeeded it in 1925), has the most inclusive membership of any of the large mission areas of the world. The Church of Christ in Congo is the name accepted by almost all of the Christians there. The other councils also are uniting the mission forces in Africa in common tasks of many kinds. In a number of the councils Africans are taking part, but in the Congo and some other areas the African participation is distressingly low. There is no end to the need of progress. That is one of the glories of the Christian religion. It is ever demanding and achieving more.

We close this book on a *sixth* element in the load North America should bear, sharing strength with Africa and the world.

Few now remember the first points made in President Truman's Washington inaugural address on January 20, 1949. There are three of them. I have read them again. They are good points.

But Point IV was something else. Point IV became a kind of flaming torch.

A flaming torch can singe and burn. There are those in our

continent who profess to fear that it will ignite and consume our substance. Our strength will be gone and the world with it. We must guard our substance to save the world.

A flaming torch can flicker and die. There are those in Europe with eyes that have seen much. Perhaps too much, more than sight can bear. With cynic eyes they mark the flicker. Perhaps the flame will die out. A torch to lighten the earth must have fuel, they say. Who pays the bill? How long? Why?

But a flaming torch can glow and beckon.

It seems probable that no other proposal of a head of state has ever called forth so quickly from so many such approbation with such hope throughout the whole world. An examination of the newspapers of January 21 and the next days, of the radio texts, of the weeklies, of all comments within the fortnight following shows an extraordinary response.

One may say: why, certainly. A billionaire give-away. What would you expect? People want it, sure.

That is a wrong judgment. As things have turned out at present with much of what is still called Point IV—with militarization, rearmament, and the stockpiling of "strategic" materials tied to such aid—many people do not want it. They have to be coerced or bribed to take it. Witness Iran. And there are others.

Let me suggest three reasons why the torch glowed and beckoned.

Point IV initially was placed upon a high level: "Bold new program . . . for the first time in history . . . help the free peoples, through their own efforts, to produce more . . . to lighten their burdens . . . a world-wide effort for the achievement of peace, plenty, and freedom . . . to benefit the peoples of the areas. . . . The old imperialism . . . has no place in . . . a program of development based on the concepts of democratic fair-

[133]

dealing. Only by helping the least fortunate of its members to help themselves can the human family achieve the decent, satisfying life that is the right of all people. Democracy alone can supply the vitalizing force to stir the peoples of the world into triumphant action, not only against their human oppressors, but also against their ancient enemies—hunger, misery, and despair."

In the human slough and smog of 1949, Point IV seemed truly to flattened and even desperate millions to be a torch that glowed and beckoned. For there was little hint of subservience in it. It suggested no coercion; but rather that there would be none. It hinted no sharp barrier of race or class, of nationality or politics. It seemed a call to all to work for all. It had this "oneness" in it. And the soul of man hungers for oneness. This was one reason why the torch glowed and beckoned.

The second reason was that it seemed to some hundreds of millions of people, Christians and non-Christians, too, who heard about it in fourscore countries of the world, many of them in direst want, that this sounded like an expanded global Christian missionary program.

For vast numbers of people, the great majority of them non-Christians, regard Christian missions as the greatest demonstration they've ever seen of selfless service to others with desirable and understandable spiritual illumination, cohesion, and power. Only a few of them have agreed to the inner personal revolution required by this spiritual power.

It is that near-universal acceptance of the products, if not the producer, of the Christian missionary program that Wendell Willkie noted, perhaps not without considerable surprise, and called America's "reservoirs of good will" in the Near East—an area where things foreign and strange and non-Islamic generally get one of the coolest receptions in the world.

[134]

Point IV in January of 1949 sounded very much like the material-producing part of the missionary program. The acceptance-minded people in all these countries would, many of them, naturally assume that it had a spiritual motivation. This was very understandable and agreeable to them since they looked to the spiritual to guide all their own private and public affairs. Hadn't they seen this same kind of thing done under obvious spiritual guidance by American Christian missionaries, and weren't Americans more or less alike—quite strange in many ways, but yet quite alike—and wasn't America a Christian country? Ergo!

Another consideration was that governmental bodies were not likely to invite anybody to accept a new religion with all the inner dislocation and community problems which that raised. So in Point IV they could have all the blessings of a Christian mission program, greatly expanded, and none of its discomforts. The world acceptance in 1949 was practically unanimous.

The third reason for this acceptance lay in the impressive fact that for the first time in history the head of a government able to do something weighty about the matter had proposed a mutually-shared task of this kind.

The memory of the billions of *things,* and the novelty and usefulness of many of them, that America had shipped and exposed and then more or less given away around the world in World War II and afterwards was very vivid. Nothing like it had been seen—so many things and all coming from one source and at practically no cost locally, except in some localities the staggering cost of war's destruction. Here was a nation powerful enough to do something in a proposed mutual effort of this sort. It sounded good.

Of course, there was the matter of this very power. Foreign power was known to be pretty selfish and greedy. Let foreign power get in and a country could lose a lot. America was foreign. But there were two or three things to consider. America had never come in and seized much political and economic power from them. And there was a lot of talk of freedom and liberty in America and by Americans. Maybe some proof, too. They seemed friends with Canada and Mexico, and they had let the Philippines go. But there was another thing—the missions and the universities and the philanthropic foundations and the Department of Agriculture and some other institutions—they must have a lot of power in America and they'd done right well with much of the world.

So Point IV had a remarkable acceptance in 1949.

What has happened since, including the bloody locked struggle in Korea and the death of Henry Garland Bennett, has profoundly altered Point IV. Under the Economic Cooperation Administration, the Point IV type of aid had to be administered quite obviously in underdeveloped colonial areas for the principal objective of restoring European economic life. Much of such aid was for great and needed public works from which the colonial peoples might eventually greatly benefit. But the ECA objective was to build up *European* economy. This was precisely what, for several generations, the colonial peoples had often bitterly accused the European colonial powers of doing. And now America was aiding and abetting this! Point IV was something very different from what they had thought. (ECA aid was not Point IV, technically. But Africans have so few technicians to unravel these things for them.)

Under the mutual security program now administering a good deal of aid, the rearmament and strategic materials aspects are stressed. There are many non-Communist nations who are not desirous at all, for a variety of reasons, of arming to the teeth. They have home needs of food and shelter and clothing and health that humanly and politically are most pressing.

They look eagerly at Point IV's concluding challenge about democracy stirring the peoples "into triumphant action, not only against their human oppressors, but also against their ancient enemies—hunger, misery, and despair." Those three are right in the house with them. If they could get them out, they could make a better stand against their other oppressors.

So now Point IV looks decidedly different in the light of 1952.

As a program of governments it has suffered the disability of governments. It gets tied to a power program. For the heart of government is power. And one government's power often clashes with another government's power, even when both want things good for both.

In Christian-based democracies it is the poeple who in the end and sometimes with agonizing slowness shape and use the power of their governments. It is the people of different countries who must learn to know and understand and trust one another. Example: Canada and the United States, where our governments' powers are formed and used under that knowledge and trust.

But this is not so today with Africa. Most governments and Africans in Africa today probably do not basically trust North American governments regarding many African matters. Colonial governments in Africa today generally do not want American government-sponsored personnel introduced there under Point IV auspices. They might desire some additional know-how and some money, but not American government personnel in any effective numbers.

Here is clearly to be seen the real and heavy load that 50 or 60 million North American Christians bear with regard to Africa and to Africa's position with the world. It involves a relation of people to people. It is a thing no governments can do at this stage. It is a thing no governments ever can aid with greatest effectiveness unless their peoples have first established a large degree of understanding and trust. It is a thing to which the Christian gospel leads us by all its teaching of God's fatherhood, of man's brotherhood, of the sharing of burdens, of the undefeatable faith, hope, and love in the hearts of men.

That real and heavy task, essential for Africa, for us, and for the world, is the creating of Christian Community in and with Africa—that Christian Community which is open not only to all peoples but which has concern for all of the life of all of the people. In such a Christian Community what has come to be called "Point IV" is a basic and historically accepted major element—the aiding of all the life of all the people. Land, food, clothing, shelter, health, religion, literacy, literature, education, communications, recreation, economics, family, community, government—all these things are, or should be, the Christian concern of Christians everywhere, for everybody. For government, that concern constituted a "bold new program . . . for the first time in history." For Christians, it is a part of the life work of every generation, placed upon us by the teaching and example of Christ 2,000 years ago. And wherever such work has been truly done since, it has lifted man and society. Where it has been best done, man and society are at their best.

Let Christians now pick up and greatly broaden their own accepted and proven mission, that great spiritual, human service on which the whole 1949 "Point IV" concept was based. That is a service in which "oneness" is basic, for it must embrace the whole of man, the whole of life.

That is a service which governments can never render in its entirety. It is a service essentially of peoples with peoples. It is a service in which the Christian dynamic has produced greater and better results than any other in human experience. It is a service for laymen everywhere, for men and women, for young and old, for clergy, for all colors and all tongues. It is for educators and farmers, for economists and engineers, for doctors and writers, for artists and lawyers, for carpenters and musicians, for veterinarians and preachers and printers and motion picture people and editors. There are things to be done, at home and in Africa, by everybody. For this deals with the whole of life. It is peoples working with peoples for the good of all people.

There is nothing visionary and "do-goody" about this. It is one of the basic, solid facts of life—of individual life, of community life, of national life, of world life. It is one of the principle things that gives Canada and the United States, separately and together, the kind of a life we like in so many of its aspects.

Let then the Christian organized bodies of Canada and the United States accept this expanding challenge for Africa. Let them greatly enlarge their already proven work for the whole of man in all of Africa—expand it, staff it in new categories, and above all in this decade encourage and accomplish a hundred-fold increase of African dynamic Christian leadership in every phase of this service.

Mr. John Foster Dulles recently called attention at Princeton to the serious lowering of our Western spiritual dynamic, and the powerful rise of Soviet communist dynamic. If our dynamic continues throttled, where shall we end?

In Africa there is a wide-open challenge. A rising people develop dynamic. Thus far the greatest dynamic in Africa is Christianity. But its position is now critical. Africans see in the West the low dynamism of Christianity, the high dynamic of communism. They note certain static elements of Christianity in

Africa, in race and color and economics and politics. They wonder. They begin to doubt.

Here is the time to advance. Here is the challenge for new Christian dynamism. The Christian dynamic started Point IV—it was a part of our mission. The Christian church initiated the experiment, gradually set the pattern by trial and error—and there were plenty of both! The world response to Point IV in the early months of 1949 was a tremendous tribute, in large part, to the scores of years and the tens of thousands of missionaries, and their supporters at home, and the millions of men and women of all colors and tongues who labored together with them, in eighty countries of the world, to accomplish Point I in their mission: together to serve men in love and faith for the saving of the whole of man, body, mind, and soul.

That is the oneness for which Christ died. That is the wholeness that man seeks. That is the profoundest need of Africa. That is the great load that North America helps to bear.

Africa has a pristine treasure. It is a sense of wholeness of life that comes, almost unaltered, from the primal days of man's creation. The West, too, has its treasures, some with vistas of joy and beauty so great that the soul is in agony to reach them. But wholeness in the West is nearly gone.

It might be, in God's good plan, that the West and Africa were timed to meet in just our day—two great hosts, the one in its primal wholeness, the other in its modern fission.

Economists say Africa is our new bread basket and ore bank. Militarists say Africa is our great field of maneuver. Politicians say Africa is our last big holding; hold it we must.

Christians can well say that Africa holds, direct from our Creator, some of this primal wholeness that we so widely seek. Let us join and aid her fully. With what we know, with what she has, with what together we can as free men do, the world may well save its soul. And all the rest shall be added; man's treasure of wholeness may be rewon. Perhaps in this there is for man the African heritage.

Bibliography

There is a wide range of literature available in most libraries both on the general history and description of Africa and its several areas. Space permits here only a brief selection of recent, available, and reasonably priced titles. For more intensive study, write for the Bibliography on Africa, 15 cents, to the Missionary Research Library, 3041 Broadway, New York 27, New York. The views of the authors represented here are not necessarily in harmony with those of the author of *African Heritage.* Leaders of adult groups studying Africa are directed to *Guide for Adults on Africa,* by Margaret Shannon. Published by Friendship Press, New York, it is available through denominational literature headquarters, price 50 cents.

Abundant Life in Changing Africa. New York, Africa Committee, Division of Foreign Missions, National Council of Churches, 1947. $1.25. Report of West Central Africa Regional Conference held at Léopoldville, Belgian Congo, in 1946. Excellent resumé of missionary work in that part of Africa.

Africa: Continent of the Future, by George Edmund Haynes. New York, Association Press, 1952. $3.50. Results of the YMCA survey that was designed to serve the youth of Africa. Contains much factual information about the various political areas of Africa.

Africa—New Focus of Unrest, by Harold Isaacs, and *Africa's need for Wholeness,* by Emory Ross. No. 91, Headline Series. New York, Foreign Policy Association, Inc., 1952. 35 cents.

Bibliography

Africa Steps Out, by Ronald K. Orchard. London, Edinburgh House Press, 1952. 3/6. Brief survey of missionary activities in certain British areas in Africa.

African Dependencies: A Challenge to Western Democracy, by Nwankwo Chukwuemeka. New York, Williams-Frederick Press, 1950. $3.50.

Attitude to Africa, by W. Arthur Lewis, Michael Scott, Martin Wight, and Colin Legum. Harmondsworth, England, 1951. 50 cents. A Penguin Book that may be obtained at many bookstores in the United States. A survey of the main problems of British Africa, suggesting the lines of policy that any British government should follow in the years ahead.

Bantu Prophets in South Africa, by Bengt G. M. Sundkler. London, Lutterworth Press, 1948. $6.50. Distributed by Friendship Press. Scholarly research in the separatist movement in the church of South Africa.

British Rule in West Africa, by Vernon McKay. Vol. 24, No. 7. New York, Foreign Policy Association, Inc., 1948. 25 cents.

A Century in Nigeria, by George W. Sadler. Nashville, Broadman Press, 1950. 60 cents. History of the Southern Baptist missionary work in Nigeria.

Cry, the Beloved Country, by Alan Paton. New York, Charles Scribner's Sons, 1948. $1.69. A beautifully written novel dealing with the difficult racial problem in the Union of South Africa.

Highways for God in Congo, by George W. Carpenter. Léopoldville, Belgian Congo. 50 cents. Jubilee brochure of Protestant missions in the Belgian Congo. Now on the press at Léopoldville. Write denominational bookstores.

I Love the Trail, by John M. Springer. Illustrated. Nashville, The Congo Book Concern, 1952. Cloth $2.50, paper $1.50. Sketch of life of Helen Emily Springer by her husband with whom she spent many years in Africa.

Last Chance in Africa, by Negley Farson. New York, Harcourt, Brace & Company, 1950. $5.00.